*Milton on America*

# MILTON
# ON
# AMERICA

*Taking the Economic Pulse
of the U.S.A.*

by **ARTHUR MILTON**

CITADEL PRESS　　　SECAUCUS, NEW JERSEY

Copyright © 1987 by Arthur Milton

Published in 1987 by Citadel Press
A division of Lyle Stuart Inc.
120 Enterprise Avenue, Secaucus, NJ 07094
In Canada: Musson Book Company
A division of General Publishing Co. Limited
Don Mills, Ontario

Queries regarding rights and permissions should be
addressed to: Lyle Stuart, 120 Enterprise Avenue,
Secaucus, N.J. 07094

Manufactured in the United States of America

ISBN 0-8065-1039-0

To My Grandchildren

Stephen
Lauren
Pamela
Melissa
Todd
Jennifer
Stephanie
Jonathan

AND ALL THE GRANDCHILDREN IN AMERICA

I dedicate this book

It is they who will carry our country's torch of freedom
into the twenty-first century

It is they who will participate in the great growth and
prosperity of the U.S.A.

It is they who will benefit from the efforts of their
forebears who preceded them

It is they who will glitter with accomplishment.

## ACKNOWLEDGMENTS

To my wife Phyllis
for her wit, companionship, intellect, love, affection and constant
understanding while I travelled throughout our country speaking
to all the people who mean so much to both of us

And to the Founding Fathers of our country who two hundred
years ago on the 17th day of September in the year 1787 gave to
all of us a Constitution so that the best country in the world
could evolve; the patriotism of all 240 million Americans is
evident in every nook and corner of our great land

And to all my friends, much too numerous to mention, who
inspired me to complete this manuscript, I thank you for your
encouragement.

# *Preface*

A T LAST we can see the light at the end of the tunnel and we can envision at no distant future the United States again becoming a strong, virile and productive nation."

Those were Arthur Milton's words in his 1983 book, *A Nation Saved: Thank You, President Reagan.*

In writing that book, Milton spent countless hours in the nation's capital, interviewing those in power in the Reagan administration. He concluded that President Reagan had succeeded in bringing about a "revolution" during his first term of office that would diminish many of the problems of the past two decades and mark the beginning of a return to greatness for this country.

The time spent in Washington was fruitful. But Arthur Milton has always been a man of the people. It was only natural that sooner or later he would go to that source to verify the beliefs he had formed during the Washington period. And that's exactly what he did. For nearly all of 1986 he traveled across America, visiting dozens of small towns and big cities throughout the nation.

The result is this book. Milton has truly taken the economic pulse of America—and Americans—and his findings are both informative and inspirational. He analyzes all the major social and economic issues of our day—inflation, jobs, population, taxes, finances, the legal system, the armaments issue, crime and drugs with the sharp eye of the investigative reporter. But, as an experienced observer of the rhythms and tides of humanity, he balances that view with an eye to the emotional side of the human condition as well. As you read, you'll feel a close bond with Arthur Milton—and with the people of America.

But Milton does more than just offer an analysis of the America of 1986. Not only does he highlight the concerns and dilemmas of families today, but he offers legitimate, practical solutions and suggestions.

Some of these suggestions are concrete, such as how families can better structure their financial planning—the personal crusade that has gained him notoriety as America's leading consumerist. Others are less specific, but just as legitimate— like his suggestion that many Americans need to turn away from the notion that "the good old days" were better, and recognize the many blessings that abound in America today.

While most people seem all too anxious to tell us what's wrong with our country, Arthur Milton tells us what's *right* about America. Milton on America is both a clear analysis of the state of the country today and an inspiring reminder of the things we ought to remember and be grateful for about this great country.

I can't think of a better, more worthwhile message to bring *to* the people of America *from* the people of America. And I can't think of a better person to carry this message than Arthur Milton. I've known Arthur Milton for five years, and I can freely say that I've never seen a man who loves his country—or its people—more. We owe him a special debt for reminding us, in *Milton on America,* that our country—with all its faults—is still the greatest country in the world.

Arthur L. Williams, Jr.
*January 1987*

# Contents

## 1. Feeling the Pulse/23

*My trips and speeches across the land . . . Americans are smarter now, they understand about savings and investments . . . they have forced banks to pay higher interest . . . They are switching to term insurance from cash value life . . . I found people disgusted with greed, moral cowardice, infantilism and cynicism in both private and public life . . . They are concerned about our national failures and the arms burden . . . They want a return to traditional ethics.*

## 2. Count Your Blessings/33

*Those who complain that American society and economy are crumbling should ask themselves why so many millions all over the world want to come here to stay . . . We do have disturbing problems, but cynicism could destroy the Republic . . . Other countries have all our problems and many others more deadly . . . Reagan's triumph over inflation is proving a big help . . . His handling of air traffic controllers' strike a turning point . . . Benefits of the big drop in interest rates.*

### 3. The Good Old Days Were Awful/45

*Food prices were cheaper before World War II but farm labor was back-breaking and soul-crushing in the horse and buggy era . . . Jobs were more plentiful but often brutal . . . Social Security and unemployment insurance were just starting on the eve of World War II . . . There were few pensions and life insurance was grossly inadequate . . . Hospitalization insurance had just started, and there was no medical coverage . . . Few anti-biotics . . . Diseases that now have been conquered were big killers . . . No air conditioning, no television and only tiny airline traffic . . . The horse and buggy days before World War I were a real horror.*

### 4. Still the Land of Opportunity/57

*Opportunities plentiful but mainly in new fields: TV, music, mass-appeal fiction . . . Also in law, medicine, accounting, some academic fields; some in insurance and investment banking . . . Always opportunities in selling . . . Not so many good chances in mining, oil, manufacturing and transportation, but building is still good.*

### 5. Keeping Our Population Balance/69

*We are almost the only nation to keep our population in balance with food supply . . . We could lose that balance if we don't solve current agricultural problems . . . Illegal immigrants and illegitimate children swelling population . . . Great American agricultural takeoff that began in the 1920s now slowing so much that Congress might have to forbid all further diversion of land from farming.*

### 6. Can Tax Reform Help?/83

*We won't know for two to three years . . . New law not a cosmetic job, it's a real change . . . It fails to attack problem of taxing underground economy . . . Do corporations really pay taxes? . . . Corporation tax rewards inefficiency and penal-*

*inefficiency on the part of military leaders and defense contractors . . . The strong dollar is the chief villain in our export decline . . . Auto industry at last is fighting back.*

## 10. Crime, Narcotics and Violence/135

*Ordinary crime is down a little but white collar crime is growing . . . So is drug trafficking and addiction . . . We blame drug traffic on foreign nations, but if Americans would stop buying and using, the traffic would dry up . . . Narcotics and alcohol figure in most violent crime and tragic accidents . . . Violent TV programs and motion pictures foster violence, so does the weak family discipline of our permissive era.*

## 11. Where We Stand/149

*We are one of the few nations not periodically or constantly threatened by revolts or military takeovers, but if our trade and overall deficits continue to grow, our political and economic prestige will fall both abroad and at home . . . Foreign trade deficit is likely to persist . . . Import quotas have failed; they enabled the Japanese to make $3 billion extra profit by selling us fewer cars at higher prices . . . Brookings economists say American steel industry wrecked itself by depending on protection quotas instead of slashing wages and other costs.*

## 12. Where to Start/159

*The place is in the home; we should manage our family and financial affairs better, thus setting an example to children . . . Parents should back teachers who are firm disciplinarians . . . Just how to proceed with family budgeting, savings and investment tactics in order to inspire respect in children and friends . . . How to plan safely for retirement.*

# *Introduction*

**F**AIRLY RECENTLY I began to notice that small retail businesses in New York City were being taken over by Indians, Arabs, Chinese, Koreans and Japanese.

In the laundromats and supermarkets one hears in addition to the expected English and Spanish the languages of these new small entrepreneurs plus a lot of Portuguese and even Turkish. Of course, one has to be curious enough to ask the people what language they are speaking. Most of those who speak Portuguese turn out to be from Brazil. In my travels around the country lecturing I discovered this is by no means unique to New York. It is happening in all our big cities and even in smaller towns. It seemed like a somewhat surprising development in our society. No longer is just New York City the world's melting pot, it is all of the U.S.A.

Then I read a newspaper feature article that was even more surprising. The article said that almost half of our legal immigrants in the last few years came from Asia and the Middle East, but what was really arresting was the news that these new immigrants are not peasants or laborers like the hordes of immigrants who came from Europe in the nineteenth century and the first quarter of this century. On the contrary, the article said, they definitely are middle-class people. They are well educated and speak English fluently *before* they leave their homelands. They have some financial reserves or their families back in the homelands do. Many come with a very definite plan to buy a business or set up in business on their own.

I suppose the migration of so many, from so many strange lands, is easier today. When my father came from Hungary in the year 1894 at the age of twelve, it took three months in steerage on a large ocean-going freighter. Today, from the remotest parts of the world, you can land in our country within twenty-four hours on a most comfortable jet plane. How all this would have astonished my father, if he was here and went with me on my travels throughout our great country in the past several years.

Others of these new immigrants come to take lucrative jobs in fields in which trained people are in short supply in the United States. They are physicians, registered nurses, college professors with specialties that are much in demand in our country, scientists, engineers and skilled technicians.

The significance of this is that America is changing more rapidly and more deeply and broadly than most of us realize. Only fifty years ago these well-to-do immigrants would not have met with a very warm welcome. The Indians and Arabs would have heard themselves referred to as wogs, the Koreans as gooks and the Chinese as chinks.

This set me to thinking that someone ought to write about the overall economic and social changes, not about the new immigrants. What I mean by an overall book is one that is not too narrow and specialized. Nearly all non-fiction books are narrow and specialized. All but one of my own previous books have been very specialized, dealing either with life insurance, the stock market, family finance or inflation. So it occurred to me that a book taking a general overview of the economy and our society, or at least of those parts of it with which I am familiar, might not be a bad thing.

Next I began to realize that I have had a rather unique opportunity in my business career to observe people's reactions to economic and social change. I have traveled around the country for over forty years and have delivered more than a thousand lectures. I have talked with an astonishing number of people on radio and TV. So I decided to write about the current economic problems and people's reactions to them as I found them.

But, a little bit more about the new immigrants. The article that fascinated me so much said most of these people spurn our big cities. They settle immediately in the affluent suburbs and the more prosperous small towns. They do not form ethnic enclaves, but move right in alongside the native born Americans as economic and cultural equals and seek to make friends with their new neighbors. They have no inferiority complexes about their homelands, whether or not they approve of the political regimes presently in power there.

It makes me wonder why our blacks, our own homebred citizens, have not more successfully integrated since the Civil War ended. There are many ways to answer this question but any one of them would get you into more controversy than I want to get into right now.

The refugees from Vietnam are an exception. Some of them settle in our larger cities but most of them form ethnic enclaves in the countryside or along the seacoasts and try to live and work here much as they and their forebears did in Vietnam for centuries.

Every week we read about examples of how crass stupidity, arrogance and irresponsibility on the part of American politicians, businessmen and tourists annoys or even infuriates people in other countries. We seem to many in the world to act as if we think of ourselves as the inheritors of the white man's burden that sustained the British and French empires for so long. We aren't. Neither are we inheritors of those shattered empires, although it must have looked to many Vietnamese as if we considered ourselves heirs of the French in their country.

What I am getting at is that we need to know a lot more about our own political and psychological strengths and weaknesses, both as a nation and as individuals. We need to realize, for example, that being born under the Stars and Stripes doesn't automatically make one more intelligent, more honest or more personable than other people anywhere in the world. So we cannot afford to go gallivanting around the planet pretending to superiority.

I am convinced that our strengths outweigh our weaknesses by far, but the rest of the world sees our weaknesses more clearly, so we need to wipe out or reduce the presumptuousness that so many people in the world consider to be the dominant trait of our national character. In order to do that we must know ourselves better.

I found on my lecture tours that Americans do know themselves better now than they did only thirty years ago, and considerably better than our immediate forebears did.

We have learned a lot of useful things.

We have learned that education does not open all the doors to success, but too many parents still labor under this delusion and push their children through college whether they are suited for it or not. Some young people embrace the notion that a college degree and a graduate degree automatically will bring a life of success and comfort so completely that they become permanent students and consider themselves successes even though they have not actually made a start on the road to success. Many others leave college, find a job and think all they have to do in order to succeed is play the game of life according to liberal rules. There is a rude awakening when they fail on their first job or are laid off because of a business recession, a merger or some other economic upheaval.

We have discovered that, indeed, education sometimes can be a barrier to success because it tells us too much about the limitations imposed by science, technology and social conditions on achievement. We all have heard of at least one case of a man or woman who made a big success out of some venture because he didn't know, as the experts did, that it couldn't be done. I know many such people. People who come from humble beginnings, lacking much formal education, yet glory in success. (Possibly my next book will be to talk about their Keys to Success as they will relate them to me.)

The universities are coming to realize this and are putting more emphasis on work study programs because work is more apt to generate original ideas than study, and to demonstrate to students that "theoretical knowledge without experience usually leads to nothing."

We have learned that in political economy, as in everyday living, you cannot eat your cake and have it. You cannot create jobs for all, keep inflation under control and hold interest rates down all at the same time. Those persons who believe that this is being accomplished in the communist countries are naive. It is their enormous police power that enables the communist countries to conceal serious economic problems and squelch any protests by the public over high prices and other hardships.

Many of us have learned that, in spite of the belief by a vast number of businessmen that the huge bargaining power of labor unions is the sole or the most important cause of inflation, that is not true. The price of labor does contribute to inflation, but there was inflation in the world long before there were labor unions. We can see now that inflation has different causes in different areas. The more we study inflation in our time, the more we are compelled to conclude that its major cause is war or the fear of war.

We also have learned that inflation is a great breeder of crime—especially racketeering and white collar crime. It also breeds political corruption.

We have learned that we cannot depend on run-of-the-mill professional politicians to provide leadership. We have to treat these people as our servants and make them do our will.

That has a serious disadvantage, however, in that it causes our representatives in Congress and the state legislatures to take a much too narrow and parochial view of their responsibilities and to pay only lip service to the general welfare.

But the most important thing we have learned is that, in spite of all our economic and social troubles, we are so much better off than our predecessors that we should be extremely thankful.

And I learned that Americans in general are convinced that our country still is the land of opportunity. The rest of the world must agree, for so many millions come here, either legally or illegally. This is the place where one has the best chance to have a good life and to accumulate something to leave to one's children. All of us in our free America can leave a legacy. The size in money is but one measure. What you have done for others along the road of life can be more rewarding.

ARTHUR MILTON

# CHAPTER 1

# *Feeling the Pulse*

FOR SEVERAL YEARS I have been travelling the United States talking to people in meetings and on radio and television about life insurance, investing and family economics.

In 1986-87 I have stepped up this activity so much and have met and talked with so many people that I find that I have actually been taking the economic pulse of America. I once spoke on a television network program that has an audience of thirty to forty million persons.

I have spoken in my home town, New York City, in Boston, Philadelphia, Charleston, West Virginia, and Morristown, New Jersey, in the east; in Atlanta, Knoxville, Tampa, Miami, Fort Lauderdale, Houston and Dallas in the south; in Chicago, St. Louis, Minneapolis and Columbus in the midwest; and in San Francisco, Oakland and Reno in the far west.

Many of these talks were simply to promote the sale of my books. Others were to spread the gospel of the vast superiority of term life insurance over old-fashioned cash value, whole life insurance.

All my talks aroused public interest and questions and comments from persons of all ages, both sexes, all kinds of ethnic origins and all kinds of vocations. When the time came for audience questions on the broadcast talks, the station switchboards lit up with incoming calls and remained lit up for long periods.

Although my talks were primarily about money matters, I found that the listeners wanted to talk about a great many other things. They were concerned about many social, political and moral trends in American life, about the foreign and domestic policies our government is pursuing. And about crime, narcotics trafficking and addiction and the mushrooming violence of our times.

Still, most of the questions were about money matters. I discovered that people all across the land are a lot smarter about these matters than they were only a few years back. In 1964 I wrote a book entitled *How to Get a Dollar's Value for a Dollar Spent*. It was an elementary treatise on saving, industriousness, understanding the true cost of living, family banking and credit, insurance, how to buy a house and get a good mortgage, how to buy everything from groceries to an automobile, taxes, wills and every other topic I could think of. The book was successful enough to attract imitators and to find its way onto the shelves of many town and school libraries.

I think the appearance of that book marked the beginning of practical comprehensive consumer education in America. Before then consumer education was almost entirely a matter of comparison shopping and quality and performance tests for everything from shoe laces to automobiles. While everything in the 1964 book is still perfectly true, I must say that if I were writing it today, it would have to be vastly more sophisticated to hold the reader's interest.

The people I talked with on my 1986-87 trips take very critical looks at everything they read or hear on broadcasts and even more critical looks at what someone is trying to sell them. My questioners revealed this by their inquiries about life insurance. For example: Since you cannot borrow on a term policy, isn't the loan value of a cash value policy a substantial plus? How can those who rely on term insurance have

any insurance protection in their twilight years since premium costs then are utterly unaffordable?

The answer to the first question is that when you borrow on
a cash value life insurance company you really are borrowing
your own money and paying someone else—the insurance
company—interest on the loan. The reply to the second question is that very few persons in their sixties and seventies
need any life insurance protection.

My listeners were impressed by the realization that you
don't lose anything if a term policy lapses—you already have
received full value in protection while it was in force. But 23
percent of all cash value, whole life policies lapse within a
year and a half after being issued, with substantial losses of
excessive premium costs to the policy holder.

Many also wanted to know if cash value, whole life insurance accumulations could be put into an Individual Retirement Account or a Keogh retirement plan. The answer is
"no," the government won't permit it, so the policyholder's
money is blocked out of IRAs, the best investment vehicle
available to Middle America today.

I also found that people are concerned about much more
than their own financial welfare. Ours has been called "the
me generation," but I learned that these people realize we all
are interdependent, and they are concerned about a lot more
than "what's in it for me?"

The sophistication of the people I encountered sometimes
made me wonder how confidence men and clever financial
operators still are able to lure millions—and make no mistake
about that, they do lure them—into sinking their money into
phony tax shelters and a wide variety of investment scams that
ought to be as transparent as the sale of gold bricks or shares
in the Brooklyn Bridge or non-existent railways, mines and
factories in the nineteenth century. The only answer I could
come up with is that greed can blind even well-educated and
sophisticated humans to obvious absurdities and falsehoods.

Detectives and accountants who specialize in catching bunco artists and big-scale white collar criminals long have said much the same thing; the easiest victim for a con man is another con man. In spite of his street smarts and street sophistication, a con man will easily take the bait that he is being "let in on the inside" of a big scam only to discover that he is being fleeced along with the other suckers.

But I don't really want to talk about con men and suckers. I want to talk about the sober honesty, candid optimism, industry, thrift and concern for the national economic, social and moral welfare I encountered in so many men and women during my travels. I found them all deeply concerned by the spread of greed and moral cowardice in the nation. They also were concerned over the spread of squandermania and extravagant living marked by so much impulse buying.

Many deplored the growth of the credit card system. They confirmed what I long have believed, that credit cards are a great evil because most people who have them cannot resist impulse buying and so cannot be sensible or reasonably thrifty in spending their incomes. They fall in debt, stay in debt and waste a big part of their earnings on high interest charges, other credit fees and credit life insurance.

The credit card thus puts many persons willy-nilly at the mercy of an artificially created sellers' market controlled by high pressure hucksters of overpriced merchandise and services, much of them of dubious value.

Many persons told me they wished they never had applied for a single credit card; the extra costs were too great and the temptations to impulse buying too hard to resist. However, expensive as it is, the credit card has become a necessity for one who travels much and a great convenience for others. It now is the only alternative to carrying dangerously large amounts of cash. Hotels, restaurants, airlines and auto rental firms take credit cards instantly but won't accept checks even with the best possible identification.

Millions of dollars are lost through credit card frauds every month, but the credit card business itself and the extra merchandise and services sales it generates are so profitable that the fraud and card theft losses are simply absorbed, further increasing the ultimate cost burden on consumers.

This is a serious matter in an economy in which most people live on a very small financial margin. After making the mortgage or rent payment on the home, the automobile and other installment loan payments, utilities, groceries, insurance, taxes, health care bills and other absolutely basic expenses, the discretionary funds left over are small no matter what the income level is. If you see a family spending as if it had huge disposable income, you can bet the income is probably illegal or the family is getting deeper in the red every month.

Most of those I talked with are well aware of this bind and would love to find ways to escape it. The simplest solution: Never use a credit card except when you are travelling.

In spite of the problems and perplexities about money, virtually all those I talked with were very optimistic about the country's present condition and future prospects. The main reason for the optimism is that they believe in "people power." They believe the people have more political, moral and financial power now than they ever had in the past and that they can wield that power effectively if they can achieve a reasonable concensus on how to use it.

People power has been successfully exerted sporadically in the United States in the past, but often, for long periods, power rested in the hands of party bosses, Wall Street financiers and entrenched local, landed and propertied interests. Their control was absolute. Our more recent elections and the vast impact of broadcasting on politics has changed that drastically. However, the cost of political campaigning is a lot higher than it was in the days of boss and class rule. So the exercise of people power depends on massive contributions from the public to popular causes and charismatic leaders. The persons I talked with in my travels are aware of this but, in spite of the financial hurdles, most of them said people power is here to stay.

The social and economic stability of the Unites States over the past two hundred years reinforces this optimistic belief in people power. We and Britain are the only really big western countries where there is no possibility of a coup d'etat or a military takeover. No one dreaming of seizing power in Washington could attract a corporal's guard of followers. The American Communist Party never has been big enough to elect a constable, much less stage a coup, and our home grown fascist movements are too tiny and farcical to rate even small headlines in the press.

It has been a hundred and eleven years since anyone in the top government circles even has been suspected of wanting to stage a coup. Secretary of War Edwin Stanton was suspected but never formally accused of masterminding the assassination of President Lincoln and plotting to seize the government, but Vice President Andrew Johnson moved promptly into the White House without any uproar.

Our economy and social structure withstood the shock and strain of the Civil War, a number of financial panics, the Great Depression of the 1930s, two World Wars, the Korean War and the morass in Vietnam without seeing the rise of a single man of the hour offering himself as a dictator.

So the people I have been talking to aren't worried about people power being squelched by any domestic authoritarian coup. They are too convinced that nearly all Americans are too passionately devoted to justice and liberty for that to happen. That conviction does not blind them to the fact that there is not enough justice and liberty in the country. They are deeply and often bitterly concerned about widely prevalent abuses of justice and liberty by people in Congress, the White House staff, the state legislatures, both federal and state courts and the police at federal, state and local levels.

I also found that people fully understand that liberty entails responsibility on the part of everyone. Responsibility grows out of several things—the character one is born with, breeding and training, education and personal experience. But most of those I talked with seemed to think quite simply that responsibility comes largely from self-discipline and self-discipline derives chiefly from adherence to traditional ethics.

Of course they mean Christian-Judaic ethics based on the Ten Commandments and the Sermon on the Mount. Not quite all but most of these precepts have stood the test of centuries. They are much the same as pure Buddhist ethics and we have a lot of Buddhists in our country now. Come to think of it, the Muslims, who also are becoming fairly numerous in the United States, venerate the Jewish Old Testament and the Christian Gospels along with Mahomet's Koran.

A return to traditional ethics seems to be what really appeals to followers of religious leaders like Jerry Falwell and Pat Robertson, although many persons obviously are attracted by their personal charisma. Others are fascinated by their theological views or their political aims. But I think that, deep down, what attracts the largest share of their followers is their vigorous espousal of a return to traditional ethics. They proclaim that all Americans must return to traditional ideas of justice, morality and personal conduct if the nation is to resolve its social, economic and political evils.

That is why so many parents are sending their children to the Christian schools being established around the country as alternatives to the public schools. These parents see many of the public schools as cesspools of irresponsible permissiveness where the administrators and teachers often do not even give lip service to our traditional ethical ideals. Many of these parents would disagree emphatically with the political ideas of the charismatic religious leaders and many don't understand or care a hoot about their theology. All they want is for their kids to grow up with firm and correct ideas about the difference between right and wrong.

People are concerned about a lot else in America. Many are very angry with our big banks for lending hundreds of billions of dollars of depositors' money to foreign governments at fantastically high interest rates to finance the purchase of unneeded armaments and highly dubious industrial developments or just to line the pockets of dictators and politicos. Many of these loans may ultimately be defaulted, most of them already have had to be renegotiated with good money thrown after bad to avert defaults. And while all these shenanigans were going on, the banks were paying their depositors a beggarly five and a half percent on passbook savings and NOW checking accounts.

While they nearly all said they were for strong defense (a few of course are confirmed pacifists and believe in disarmament and strict neutrality), everyone I talked to agreed on several evil aspects of our defense system. It is much too costly and burdensome and is riddled with extravagance, fraud and incompetence. The terrible bungling of the hostage rescue attempt in Iran during the Carter administration and the incredibly sloppy handling of the invasion of the little island of Grenada have angered and humiliated millions of Americans. The invasion of Grenada probably was politically necessary but it was not necessary to waste so much time, so many lives and so much material and reveal to the world just how inefficient our military and naval establishment has become.

Other things about our defense system anger and humiliate Americans. The arrogance and obvious intellectual, professional and moral shortcomings of many generals and admirals in their dealings with greedy defense contractors and their unwieldy, inefficient organizations also humiliate and alarm civilians. So does the failure of so many costly new weapons and weapon systems to come anywhere near living up to the claims their sponsors and producers made for them. The stubborn manner in which the brass hats and the defense department bigwigs persist in continuing to finance and buy these lame ducks and outright lemons disgusts the public.

Others talked to me about our inability so far to do any thing effective about narcotics trafficking and addiction. That brings me back to the matter of traditional ethics. It's as plain as the nose on your face that if we stopped buying and using marijuana, cocaine and heroin the traffic soon would drop off. Defenders of the drug culture can talk all they want to about drugs being no worse than alcohol, but it just isn't true. Alcohol is not one-hundredth as destructive to the human body and brain as any narcotic. It is not highly addictive either; most people who use it can go weeks without a drink. Tobacco is much more addictive. Alcoholics are not addicted to alcohol, they are allergic to it.

The real solution to the drug evil, the people I talked to said, lies in persuading our people and particularly our young people to have the gumption and moral fortitude to reject drugs, and that requires, first of all, a return to traditional ethics.

Although they have discovered that we can live a number of successive years with huge annual federal deficits, including foreign trade deficits, enjoying government largesses and passing the ensuing debt on to our children and grandchildren, most people are becoming very alarmed about the situation. How, some asked me, could our manufacturing industries, only twenty years ago the finest in the world, have become unable to compete either in foreign markets or on our home soil?

Understandably, our farm exports were hurt by the em-

bargo on grain shipments to Russia because of the brutal Soviet invasion of Afghanistan, but many people cannot see how
on earth a country that only a quarter century ago was feeding
much of the human race now finds its agriculture in total disarray with millions of farmers deserting or being forced off the
land. How could we possibly fall to the point of importing
more farm products than we send abroad?

The people I talked with didn't have any precise or sophisticated answers to these questions but they were sure about
one thing—we have wrecked our agriculture by being short-
sighted and letting greedy, unscrupulous industrialists and
land speculators take too much land out of farming. They said
that if this isn't stopped we will find ourselves going hungry in
the not too distant future.

But my overall conviction is that Americans believe this
country still has a great future and they are quite willing to
struggle and fight for that future. They believe people power
will make them invincible in the struggle.

The optimistic thinking of most people across our land
portends the continuation of a stronger nation where freedom
is translated into happiness for all.

CHAPTER 2

# *Count Your*
# *Blessings*

**F**OR SEVERAL YEARS now it has been fashionable to wail and complain that American society is crumbling, particularly the nation's economy.

Those who take this pessimistic view really need ask themselves only one question, and if they answer it honestly they will have to admit that they are indulging in arrant decadence and defeatism. The question is—Why do so many persons from all over the world still clamor to get into our country and why do so many illegal aliens cross the Mexican and Canadian borders to get here?

The response has to be that things aren't so bad here after all.

There are things to be disturbed about. We have a horrendous annual foreign trade deficit, even our farm experts lately have been falling behind our agricultural imports. Some of our traditionally most important industries, steel for example, have almost been driven to the wall and our once world dominant automobile business has lost a third of its market to foreign cars, especially Japanese vehicles.

Almost every week brings news of massive factory layoffs as

many of our biggest companies cut back sharply on production, closing plants and sometimes wiping out entire divisions abruptly. The bankruptcy rate of middle- and small-sized businesses is extremely high and some industrial and financial giants have gone under. We are waging a losing battle against the narcotics traffic and drug addiction.

Our military outlays are excessive and burdensome and the defense industries and the Pentagon are repeatedly wracked by waste and corruption scandals.

It is popular to blame everything on the machinations of our rival nations, the Russians and Japanese, and on the Latin-Americans who undoubtedly do control the vast traffic in cocaine and marijuana brought to our shores illegally. This propensity to blame all our troubles on others may be the most disturbing thing of all because it tends to vitiate our belief that we can overcome the difficulties and our will power to grapple with them earnestly. It encourages a drift in the American people toward individual irresponsibility, moral cowardice, greed and cynicism.

There is nothing new in human history about trying to shift the blame for individual and national shortcomings onto someone else. The ancients had the most convenient scapegoats, the gods and the stars, for they were great believers in astrology. In *Julius Caesar,* Shakespeare has the conspirator Cassius refuse this self-serving scapegoat philosophy by saying: "The fault, Dear Brutus, is in ourselves, not in our stars, that we are underlings." Most Romans did believe the stars were responsible for nearly all disasters and failures.

The cartoon character Pogo the 'Possum put it even better than Shakespeare a few years ago with the comment, "I have seen the enemy and he is us."

But if the scapegoat propensity is old in the story of mankind it is somewhat new in the United States, at least on a national scale. Until very recently most Americans were firmly convinced, even in the face of evidence to the contrary, that they and the nation held their destiny in their own hands. They acknowledged that they were fortunate in having the wealth and resources of this vast new country and in the light of such good luck they also acknowledged that all shortcomings and failures had to be their own fault.

What are these evils that so many of us wink at, persuading ourselves that they do not arise out of our individual personalities or national character?

Greed comes to mind first. The greed that is so pervasive in America today is characterized by excessive love of luxury and excessive lust for power and prestige. Greedy persons also are excessively self-centered. This is widely recognized; more than a decade ago, authors, media commentators and clergymen bewailed the fact that we had become what they called "the me generation," that we had lost all social and political ideals and no longer pretended to be generous or even fair in our dealings with others, even with our own relatives. Parents evaded responsibility for their children and children would not care for parents in distress—that was the government's duty.

However, the worst manifestations of greed in America today are seen in business institutions, banks, insurance companies, Wall Street houses, defense contractors, oil companies, pharmaceutical houses and other manufacturers. This kind of greed leads naturally to corruption in both business and government. We have only to look at the newspapers any day to see how widespread the corruption has become. It has penetrated the learned professions, particularly the law.

Union leadership, especially in unions of blue-collar service workers, also has been shaken by corruption.

Moral cowardice is another widespread evil in our society. Persons who are physically very brave, soldiers, sailors, athletes and workers in dangerous occupations, can be moral cowards. The two aspects of moral cowardice that cause the

most trouble are fear of responsibility and fear of getting involved. The person who sees a crime being committed but
turns his head and walks rapidly away without even reporting
what he has seen to the police for fear of getting involved is a
moral coward.

However, fear of responsibility is the more dangerous evil
for the nation. This fear certainly has widened in America in
our time, particularly since the war in Vietnam. When Harry
Truman pointed to his desk and said, "The buck stops here,"
he was serving notice that he did not intend to succumb to
moral cowardice. But a rather large portion of our politicians
are moral cowards. Moral cowardice also is rampant in the bureaucracy, fairly prevalent in the higher echelons of military
and naval officers and among clergymen, educators and the
other professions. But it is rarely encountered in the medical
field; physicians simply don't have time to evade responsibility.

One of the genuine defects of bigness in business is that
bigness fosters moral cowardice in executives, and the higher
up the ladder we look the more moral cowardice we will find
hiding behind various façades. The upper business world has
lots of authoritative poseurs. The aura of success and sophistication these high-pressure executives and tycoons manage to
convey often covers extreme timidity and indolence—moral
cowardice.

Businessmen who are moral cowards sometimes give themselves protective covering by being extremely active and
brave physically; they are great hunters and big game
fishermen, expert horsemen, intrepid yachtsman and even
explorers.

It is a combination of moral cowardice, greed and infantilism that encourages so much rampant extravagance, arrant
fraud and frightful inefficiency in the armed forces and the defense industries.

Our planet is dotted with the ruins of vanished civilizations and nations. We don't even know the names of some of them or what their people looked like. But one thing we do know, they all were destroyed by infantilism, either their own or the infantilism of a rival power; usually both sides were infantile.

Infantilism is growing in the world today and it is spreading in America. It has many manifestations. The psychology of the "me generation" is the epitome of infantilism. As for the vanished civilizations, we know from meager records that their peoples never grew up sufficiently to be able to cope with such problems as overpopulation, denuded and deteriorated soil with resulting famines, or with the troubles caused by human passions, greed, arrogance, vanity, superstition, lust and love of cruelty. This is true even though there undoubtedly were men of genius in these ancient nations.

Of course, they perished for a variety of reasons, but underlying all the reasons was an infantile inability to conceive of any way of handling a problem except by slaughtering and enslaving their neighbors.

Infantilism should not be confused with naïveté. Naïve persons are simply uninformed and inexperienced, they may be quite mature both intellectually and emotionally. On the other hand many infantile persons are well educated, experienced and appear to be sophisticated. Infantilism appears to be a deep-seated personality trait. Its chief characteristics are self-concentration, irresponsibility and inability to comprehend and observe mature ethical standards. Virtually all criminals are infantile, no matter how "smart" they appear to be. All terrorists are infantile. Even though some of them are sophisticated idealists, their fanaticism discloses the underlying infantilism.

Modern infantilism causes many men and women to fall prey to false idealism and to religious, political and economic ideas that seem obviously delusionary to persons with mature personalities. Infantilism can be found in every level of American society and in every business profession. It is particularly rife in vocations that have a *deformation professionelle* such as the law and the judiciary. The people in the legal profession often appear to be divorced from the rest of us because they live in their own world created by "legal fictions" invented by clever but infantile minds over the centuries. Fortunately for me I have known many in this profession who are quite practical and business-like and personable and honest.

Infantilism causes poor judgment at any level, in single young people, in running a home and maintaining a family, getting along with the boss and holding your job, practicing a profession or operating a business. Because even well-educated infantile persons may be inclined to hysteria and tantrums, the infantile person who climbs the ladder in business may cause a vast deal of harm when he or she reaches the top.

The sex revolution has given free rein to another infantile group, the womanizers and nymphomaniacs. I don't need to expatiate on the misery and carnage caused by sexual obsession.

Narcotics addicts are infantile. Like children, they seek solace from problems and terrors in "candy." That is why the police sometimes call heroin and cocaine "nose candy."

Juvenile delinquents and adolescents who are extremely unruly are engaging in infantile behavior even though they may not actually be infantile personalities. Some illiterate persons display infantile behavior, reacting emotionally simply because they haven't the information to enable them to understand or cope with a problem.

Problem drinkers often behave in an infantile manner, but the true alcoholic may not be infantile at all. He or she is the victim of a disease of unknown origin that makes the patient allergic to alcohol.

The abandonment or abuse of children usually is infantilism at its absolute worst. Of course, the parent who abuses or abandons kids may be a victim of other disorders such as retardation or incipient schizophrenia.

Most television entertainment and many motion pictures are infantile. How much infantilism is involved in the rock 'n' roll music craze is quite a question but it's a lot—perhaps more on the part of those who listen than among the men and women who strum the guitars and blare out the lyrics. The music itself is infantile and so are many of the songs.

It seems rather natural for teenagers to listen to rock 'n' roll, but what are we to think when we see and hear grown up office and shop workers listening to it for hours on end?

However, infantile entertainment is comparatively harmless except for hardcore pornography, which may have a direct impact on the rate of sex crimes and other violent crime. Not everyone will agree with this statement; many of us think ordinary, non-sex-related violence in infantile TV programs also has a very deleterious effect on many viewers.

The overall growth of infantilism makes for weaker families, less effective schools, weaker courts and soft and poor administration in business and in government.

Whether greed, corruption, moral cowardice and infantilism causes cynicism or cynicism causes them is like the old puzzle of the chicken and the egg. The loss of our national innocence during World War II caused only mild dismay at the time, and the dismay soon was brushed aside by the prosperity and general feelings of pride and satisfaction Americans enjoyed in the early post-war years.

The cynicism set in after the Korean War and spread rather fast during the war in Vietnam. The prevalence of cynicism is the worst social ailment in the country today. Cynicism has caused many of us to lose faith in the ideals the founding fathers set for us and has destroyed many people's belief that democratic government really can work in the long term. Above all, it is casting doubt on our cherished tradition that we are a nation governed by laws and not by men with their lusts for power and wealth.

If this trend to widespread cynicism is not reversed it can easily and rather quickly destroy the republic, for it will accelerate the growth of all the other ills. Cynics have been feared and despised throughout history because whenever and wherever they have flourished decadence and a deluge of disasters soon have appeared. Fiction writers, psychologists and communists do talk sometimes of "a healthy cynicism," but what they really mean is a healthy skepticism, an absence of naïve folly. The skeptic differs from the cynic because he cares. The cynic neither believes in nor cares about his fellow man. It is this lack of caring rather than the inability to believe that deprives the true cynic of ethics, morality or social or national self-esteem and pride. The true cynic is a useless and noxious weed.

That brings me back to the question I posed at the start of the chapter. If things are going so badly in America, why do so many hundreds of thousands of people all over the world come here to live and work and why do so many millions more yearn to come?

A substantial number come to make a stake in a few years or even in a few months and then return to their homelands. But most of the immigrants, legal and illegal, remain, and most of them turn out to be industrious and law abiding. They are not greedy, they are not moral cowards and are no more subject to infantilism, corruption and cynicism, and perhaps less so, than persons whose ancestors came here three hundred years ago.

Again, why do they come? It is not easy to raise the money to get here, to learn English, to find work and to adjust to new customs and social conditions. The answer must be that all the evils I have been talking about and many others more deadly and more terrifying are much more widespread in their homelands than in America.

I do not pretend to know enough about life in the communist countries to comment on how much greed, corruption, moral cowardice, infantilism and cynicism exist in their populations, but it is undeniable that the Marxist governments have to use the sternest police tactics, Big Brother spying and harsh laws ruthlessly enforced to keep their populations from pouring out over their borders.

Our economic lead over the rest of the world is not what it was from the end of World War I to the mid-1970s. Switzerland and Sweden may enjoy higher average standards of living than we do. Canada, Australia, New Zealand, Finland, Holland and West Germany are about even with us, but we still are well ahead of the rest of the world. However, comparing national living standards can be risky. Geography makes great differences in peoples' wants and needs. For example, in tight little countries like England, Belgium and Holland an automobile may be an expensive nuisance instead of a necessity as it is in most of America. In the United States, Canada and Australia, if you don't have wheels you might as well stop breathing.

It should be pointed out that many of the foreign countries that are currently very prosperous do not have big defense burdens. They and other strategically important countries depend largely on the United States for defense.

Thanks to President Reagan's policies, we have enjoyed in recent years just about the lowest rate of inflation in the world and probably the least inflation of any country with a free economy.

The Reagan administration's feat in getting our inflation down to an annual rate of 1.5 percent for several successive months in 1982 after the severe inflation of the Carter era seems in retrospect almost miraculous. Of course, the rate could not be held at such a tiny figure, but inflation has been under very firm control all through the Reagan years.

One thing that helped bring this about is not given

sufficient credit. That is the President's handling of the illegal air traffic controllers' strike in August, 1981. By firing the nine thousand strikers after giving them a grace period to return to work, Mr. Reagan served notice that his administration would not tolerate illegal strikes of public workers but would fire the strikers no matter how much inconvenience that caused government, business and the public.

That broke the unacknowledged alliance of union leaders, politicians and management executives to let wages spiral up indefinitely and rapidly and pay for them by ever more inflation. Throughout the nation's economy, in the public sector and in the private sector, union wage demands have moderated and settlements have been more reasonable ever since the air traffic controllers' strike was broken.

Interest rates have been halved from the record levels of the Carter era. The Federal Reserve System's discount rate currently is down to 6 percent, a figure that approaches the historical levels of our stable and prosperous years. The prime lending rates of banks and other interest rates have fallen accordingly.

That means that capital is becoming available for businesses to expand and for the founding of new businesses that will create new jobs. Incidentally, we know now that our officially reported unemployment rates are unrealistically high because a substantial portion of the supposedly unemployed are working in the underground economy and are being paid "under the table."

The drop in interest rates in 1986 brought us into a deflationary era, although much of the public did not soon feel the impact of the deflation. One example: There has been a stampede of homeowners and other property owners to the banks and other lending institutions to get their mortgages refinanced at lower interest rates compared with the astronomical rates charged on new mortgages during the big real estate boom.

The collapse of the speculative real estate boom is costing a lot of people huge amounts of money; however, that's the risk people who speculate in a boom of any kind take. But on balance, the collapse of the speculative real estate boom is good news for Americans. It should, in the long run, help create a trend toward more affordable homes and commercial properties instead of luxury homes at sky-high prices and sky-high speculative prices for commercial properties.

The general public does not pay overmuch attention to the official consumers' price index. The methods by which the index is drawn up seem over-complicated and too mysterious to ordinary folk and they suspect that the bureaucrats are fiddling the figures. Instead, people go by how much they have to pay for the week's supply of groceries, by whether supermarket clerks are marking prices up or down, and whether the stores' stocks are expanding or contracting. If prices and interest rates are declining, the stores can afford larger and more diversified stocks. When prices and interest rates are high, they have to trim inventory.

People also go by how many genuine bargains they encounter in department stores, specialty stores and discount stores. In 1986, things were starting to go very much in favor of the consumers.

Can you think offhand of any other country where this is true?

So we are much better off than most of the world and we are enormously better off than our parents and grandparents were, so we should stop complaining and count our blessings.

But counting our blessings out loud or in print is after all a rather passive way to pursue a goal. We need something more dynamic. We need to get our schools to take a much more positive approach to teaching kids about the perils of greed, infantilism and moral cowardice. And we need substantial reform in the attitudes of workers, business and professional men, bureaucrats and politicians.

CHAPTER 3

# *The Good Old Days Were Awful*

**H**OW MUCH better off are we than our parents and grandparents? I heard a lot about that from many people during my speechmaking travels. They said, for the most part, that youngsters now in their late teens and twenties aren't much better off than their parents were at their age and may be worse off. Their parents' prime years were in the affluent 1950s and 1960s.

Others pointed out that we are an aging populace, so many of us were children during the Great Depression of the 1930s or even in the 1920s. There are plenty of octogenarians in America. They were born in the horse and buggy era before World War I and their parents lived and raised their kids in that economic and social climate. Plenty of us now living knew and loved grandparents who grew up in the latter part of the nineteenth century. In general, these middle-aged and elderly persons are a great deal better off than their parents and grandparents were.

We do have a problem now with impoverished elderly persons, but they do get Social Security benefits and can have their own homes. Before World War II, the impoverished elderly either lived with their children or younger siblings as dependents or in the Poor House, a county or township charity home almost as bad as the early nineteenth-century English "workhouses" described by Charles Dickens in his novels.

Very few American men were able in the so-called good old days or even in the recent past to leave their wives with anything faintly resembling financial security, whether the husbands died young or lived to a ripe old age.

Most men had a life insurance policy of some kind, but the death benefit frequently barely covered the final medical and hospital bills and the funeral expense. Today, a rather young man who dies suddenly may leave his wife a term life insurance policy with a death benefit of more than $500,000 at affordable rates.

Food was much more plentiful and a lot cheaper in the good old days than now, but it was produced by back-breaking, soul-crushing labor that created conditions in some areas no better than the serfdom and subjection of peasants to the aristocracy and gentry in the Old World. Farm laborers and even farm proprietors were subject to horrible accidents and many illnesses seldom seen today, with few doctors and no hospitals available to much of the rural population. They had no electricity, no gas, no central heat, no running water and no outside plumbing or adequate sewage disposal. These brutal conditions lasted into the 1940s in some parts of the country.

Until the depression that began after the Wall Street collapse of 1929, business slumps generally were brief, lasting only a few months. Therefore, jobs were much more plentiful than now, but once the Great Depression got firmly underway jobs became a lot scarcer and there was no significant amount of unemployment insurance available. There was very little public welfare assistance of any kind until after the Social Security Act was put in effect in 1935.

Quite a number of those I talked with on my travels lived during the Great Depression as I did and we agreed that its severity cannot even be imagined by today's young people. It lasted a full decade and changed American society forever. The financial losses in the securities and commodities markets were tremendous for the time and by historical standards. One-sixth of all the businesses in the country went broke and unemployment hit an official rate of 16 percent. All that most of the jobless could hope for, aside from help from their relatives, was assistance from a few municipal and religious welfare agencies that were not designed or prepared to deal with problems so staggering.

Young people roamed the country, hitchhiking up the highways or riding unlawfully in empty box cars on freight trains, hoping to find some kind of work at the next town. Often they got a week in jail for vagrancy instead.

The harsh times caused the defeat of President Herbert Hoover in 1932 and ushered in Franklin Delano Roosevelt's New Deal, which alleviated many bad conditions but achieved real solutions to only a few of the big problems.

But I think, and so did the acquaintances I made during my travels, that the Great Depression had its good side too. Every now and then I catch myself thinking it would have been better for my own children if they had grown up in the depression. It was a chastening experience and it taught youngsters the need for the kind of self-discipline and responsibility so many people talked to me about on my recent travels.

Even people who managed to find work had to live frugally during the Great Depression. Many families had to double up for years in order to maintain a house. But I think people often were happier then than the young people of today are. There was no significant drug evil, rather little crime and very little sexual promiscuity; comparatively few illegitimate children were born in the depression years. There were many fewer psychological illnesses.

The depression brought people together, made families closer knit and more united and did the same for entire communities. I see some signs of this in our present recession. For example, the way farmers in other states rallied to help farmers in the south in the 1986 drought by shipping them hay to save their cattle herds.

Before the depression, jobs were rather plentiful, much more so than now, but many of the jobs were miserable, paying bare subsistence wages, with rugged working conditions and mean bosses. Job security was quite marginal, often non-existent. Pensions were rare, only governmental employees, railway workers, and war veterans and professional soldiers and sailors could hope for them in general.

Things were a lot worse in the horse and buggy era than in the 1920s. My father's experience was typical. He arrived in this country in 1894 at the age of twelve, and a year later he was delivering bread and rolls with a horse-drawn cart in lower Manhatten for $3 a week—a seven-day work week. Jobs in mining, steelmaking, chemical works, many kinds of manufacturing, lumbering, seafaring and other industries were very hazardous, and compensation for death or injury usually was niggardly.

Many youngsters dropped out of high school and even grammar school, not out of waywardness like our dropouts today, but because they had to go to work to help keep a roof over the family and put food on the table.

Affordable rental housing was available all across the land in ample quantity right down to 1946, but a lot of the housing was pretty bad. Many urban tenement flats were firetraps. Some of these are still standing and still are the sites of horrible flaming tragedies. The tenements had running water and gas and some had central heating. They were uninsulated, so were hot as Hades in summer and far from warm in winter. The rooms were small and dark even on bright, sunny days.

They were badly ventilated and infested by roaches and other vermin.

Many single-family houses, even those in the cities, were jerry-built and those in the villages had no amenities, not even running water or sanitation facilities. They also were uninsulated. Water had to be drawn up from wells and heated on round galvanized iron laundry tubs. Heating the rooms was by coal-fired grates and base burner stoves, and kerosene lamps provided most of the lighting. In the cities, illuminating gas was available and electric lighting was coming into use.

Soft coal gave plenty of heat but it was messy to handle and hauling out the ashes was an arduous daily chore. Even in steam-heated houses, attending to the coal-fired furnace was rugged and tedious. The fire had to be banked at night and made up early in the morning, and the ashes raked out and hauled. Floors were of wood and hard to scrub and keep painted or waxed.

The vacuum cleaner was a luxury. The telephone was becoming affordable to all except the poorest families. Electric refrigeration didn't become common until the late 1920s. Before that, the ice man had to come every day. Very poor families had no icebox at all.

Power mowers, washing machines and driers, other electric household appliances and power tools were just beginning to appear on the general consumer market on the eve of World War II.

There was little hospitalization and virtually no medical insurance in either the horse and buggy era or the 1920s. Doctors and hospitals were plentiful (but not for black people) and they were cheap by our modern standards. Medicine and surgery were still more arts than sciences and only a few doctors got rich. The rest toiled long hours to make a modest living. Many had shabby offices and shoddy practices and struggled charging $1 to $3 per visit to a patient's house or their office.

The doctors who did get rich did so by soaking wealthy patients and telling them frankly, "You're paying for twenty poor patients I can't collect from."

Until the sulfa drugs came out in the early 1930s there were no quick cures for anything; millions died of ailments that today are treated successfully and quickly—tuberculosis, syphilis, diphtheria and pneumonia, for example. Millions of women died in childbirth. The mortality rates in surgery were very high compared with those of today.

They didn't have to contend with AIDS in those days, though.

Hospitals didn't have the good reputation they have now; in the horse and buggy era if a patient got sick enough to be sent to a hospital the family immediately started scraping together the money to pay for the funeral.

Doctors had to make house calls, often at ungodly hours of the night, in freezing weather or blinding rainstorms. Many doctors had to worry almost as much about caring for their buggy horses as about caring for their patients. That's undoubtedly why physicians became the new automobile industry's first regular customers.

Recently some research surveys have been published indicating that a significant proportion of today's middle-aged physicians are getting disenchanted with the profession and want to get out. The reasons given are that government agencies and insurance companies are getting tougher and tougher about paying claims, taking an average of two and a half months to pay, and are demanding much stricter accountability on the part of the doctors. The doctors don't like having their word doubted and having to do so much more paper work. They don't like being at last put in the position of no longer being able to unilaterally fix the size of their fees and having the need for some of the services they provide or order questioned.

But the surveys point out that most doctors have been getting very rich since the start of the medical and social revolution that followed World War II.

Their disenchantment over the crackdowns would impress the public more if so many physicians had not been indicted in recent years for filing false Medicare and other insurance claims—claims for services never performed and for services for non-existent patients—or if so many doctors had not become involved in narcotics.

Perhaps these disenchanted middle-aged physicians should count their blessings instead of griping. Perhaps they should look back at what their predecessors had to contend with. They complain at having to wait two and half months to be paid. Their forebears had to wait six months to a year sometimes and probably never collected a good quarter of their billings. But the doctors of the past did not have the malpractice insurance crisis to bear with. Yet many of my friends in the medical profession do live up to the high standards required of them. Many of them are just as concerned as I that all Americans benefit from the scientific progress in medical care.

Some of the persons I talked with recalled that in many parts of the country public schools were run on a shoestring basis and teachers' pay was excruciatingly low even in the 1930s. Naturally, the curriculum was very narrow under such circumstances. I can recall one of my public school teachers whom I envied as a young boy because his annual salary was $1500.

Travel was expensive and arduous for our forebears. A trip to California or Florida or to a metropolis like New York, Chicago or Washington was a once in a lifetime affair for even well-to-do families. Airline travel didn't become widely affordable until the 1950s. Today, the airliner makes it possible for anyone to tour Europe.

Most people had to travel by train or automobile in the old

days and both were slow and tedious and by no means cheap. Few people could spare enough time from work to travel at such a leisurely pace.

Many of those I talked with recalled how uncomfortable the trains were. They jounced and bounced and they were not air-conditioned and often were cold or overheated in winter. The locomotives burned coal and rained soot and cinders into the passenger coaches, soiling or even ruining clothing. "It was tough to get the cinders out of your hair," some oldsters recalled.

Things at home weren't much better. There was no residential or office and shop air-conditioning. This was about the most-remarked-on remembrance of the good old days. The absence of air-conditioning was tougher on men than on women because masculine attire for summer remained heavy and uncomfortable. The women had rebelled and adopted more sensible garments in the flapper era of the early 1920s. In the horse and buggy era, everybody, both sexes of all ages, had to wear long johns in winter. In those days a girl or women who appeared on the streets in a costume like many we see every day would have risked a fine or even a few days in jail.

Educational opportunities were vastly fewer. There were many fewer colleges, and scholarships and student loans were hard to come by. There were no government guaranties for student loans. Curricula were not nearly so broad as they are today and were not generally geared to teaching youngsters something immediately salable in the job market but to the basics of science and the humanities.

People I talked with thought the broadening of the curricula is a great plus for our times. The high schools today have done the same as the colleges.

Discipline at all stages of education was a lot better in the good old days. Teachers and administrators did not have to reckon with the drug culture or with the modern propensity of parents to back up unruly students and even sue teachers for disciplining them. In the horse and buggy era a kid who got a licking at school was likely to get another one when he got home.

But in addition to the broadening and deepening of the curricula, today's schools and colleges offer more opportunities than could be dreamed of in the old days because we have TV, educational films, videotapes, personal computers and so many other new educational tools. In spite of the widely known weaknesses in our schools and colleges, the children who want to learn today can learn much faster and more easily than their parents and grandparents could. I can attest that educational programs and talk shows on radio and television and now cable networks are educating the American consumer as never before.

Commercial television and public television also have an enormously favorable impact on education in spite of the efforts of the networks to avoid it and in spite of all commercial TV's bad aspects.

Today youngsters have the opportunity to learn and earn to help defray college tuition in schools that have work-study programs. One such college is in New York City, the College of Insurance, which was sponsored by twenty-one insurance firms, including my own, some twenty-five years ago.

Now if we could only harness students into high gear motivation this generation could help send our country into an orbit of great progress.

In the horse and buggy era, entertainment was church sociables, picnics, hay rides and the like, baseball and football games and just sitting on the verandah drinking lemonade and talking. People also stood around the piano and sang or listened to tinny records played on the newly invented phonograph.

There was a lot of reading, but books were expensive and fiction generally prissy. There were also Chautauqua lectures and vaudeville in the towns, but few could hope to see an opera or ballet performed, or a Broadway stage play or see a major league baseball game or a big-time football contest. They had to read about those events, or hear them described by radio announcers in the 1930s.

Then suddenly all these delights and nearly everything interesting that happened anywhere in the world could be seen and heard at first hand on television. Admittedly, a lot of TV entertainment is bad, perhaps most of it, but the sheer quantity of it and such standouts as a performance of *Carmen* by the Metropolitan Opera, a Shakespeare play, and the opportunity to see astronauts walking on the moon mean that the availability of entertainment in our town is light years ahead of anything people could enjoy in the past.

Is the sex revolution a plus or a minus for our era? The liberation of women from political and economic subjection was a great social and moral advance. Today's women and girls can count their blessings over that. But the permissiveness created by the sexual revolution is a much more complicated and clouded story. The permissiveness had its beginning in the enrollment of so many women in the armed forces during World War II, but what made permissiveness for both sexes explode all over the land was the development of successful birth control pills. Freed of the age-old fear of unwanted pregnancy, young people could indulge in sexual relationships without marriage or much responsibility.

Many women resorted to promiscuity. Many became unwed mothers and reared their illegitimate children alone. Men felt less responsibility sometimes for these children because, they reasoned or rationalized, the mothers easily could have prevented the pregnancy.

In their grandmothers' time, an illegitimate child was nearly always taken away from the mother and given to a relative, a close friend or an orphanage to rear. Only black women reared their own illegitimate kids. The stigma of illegitimacy was harsh always on the mothers and frequently on the children. White men seldom acknowledged an illegitimate child even if ordered by a court to pay for its support. Today, even if he does not feel he is to blame for the birth, the father usually acknowledges an illegitimate child at once, and that's certainly a forward step and blessing.

Most of the people I talked to were strongly opposed to the promiscuity, the permissiveness the sex revolution has bred, but some welcomed the new freedom from old rigid sexual mores and bonds.

I am impressed by the reasoning of a young woman who wrote to Ann Landers, saying, "Our mothers and grandmothers were right." She said females still should keep their virginity until marriage and should mate for life. She went on to defend the traditional double standard of sexual morality, saying it made for much stronger and more enduring families, better rearing of children and a generally stronger society than we have today under the permissive climate.

Many people today do not realize how far we have moved from the ideas on sexual morality that prevailed in the horse and buggy era. In much of the United States we still had the "unwritten law" then. If a girl was seduced, her father could kill the seducer without fear of prosecution. In some areas it was considered that he had a bounden duty to do so and he was scorned by his neighbors as a coward if he failed to kill the seducer.

Similarly, a husband had the right, even the obligation, to kill his wife's partner in adultery. The erring wife generally was forgiven, perhaps after a thrashing in private. Women were rarely divorced for adultery then, men nearly always were if they got caught. In reality, they were divorced not for the adultery itself but for humiliating the wife publicly by getting caught.

I think we can say for sure that the lapse into limbo of the unwritten law is a big plus for our times.

The mere mention of sex in mixed company could mar
one's reputation and do serious harm to a career as well as to
one's social status in those days. The main reason so many
wives were forgiven for adultery was that few men would un-
dergo the humiliation of going into court and revealing that
their wives had even dreamed of cavorting with another man.

Actually nearly all American females were uncom-
promisingly virtuous in sexual matters because for many the
only available alternative lifestyle was prostitution. Prostitution was a little less rugged then than now because few prosti-
tutes were hooked on drugs; they didn't have to earn so much
money. In view of the unfailing virtue of nearly all females,
prostitution did fill a social need in the horse and buggy days.

Most black persons are rightfully much more concerned
about the blessings they still have not attained than those they
have gained in recent decades. But to any objective eye it is
clear that these gains are enormous and could not have been
foreseen by ordinary folk as recently as forty years ago.

The racial integration of the armed forces by President
Truman during the Korean War was the biggest single step
forward. After that, black people moved on to win great victories on the most important political and economic issues that
had kept them suppressed for generations. Of course these
victories have not been consolidated and capitalized on yet,
and it still is not possible to predict when they will achieve
absolute equality of opportunity and accomplishment.

The cause for equality will only move forward from today
through improved leadership within our black society.

But all Americans can rejoice and be deeply thankful that
we did not have to pass our lives in the good old days.

CHAPTER 4

# Still the Land of Opportunity

ONE THING most of those I talked with on my travels agreed on is that America is still the land of opportunity.

However, they said the opportunities are not the same as in the past, fewer fortunes are being made nowadays in mining, oil and gas exploration and development or in manufacturing and transportation and distribution. A pop 'n' mom store is no longer a salable going concern when the time comes for pop and mom to retire.

But fantastic fortunes are being made by those acting in, writing and directing TV shows, by pop music performers, composers and songwriters, and by writers of mass-appeal fiction. All of these activities require talent. Talent with mass appeal clearly is the quickest road to wealth in America today. Furthermore it's a road open to people from even the bottom most levels of our society. The number of impoverished black youths who have become rich out of pop music is almost unbelievable.

All these talent fields also afford opportunities to some who don't have talent but have practical business sense and are willing to work very hard at managing performers or by producing, distributing and marketing phonograph records, albums, tapes, cassettes and videotapes and disks. The people with talent have to work hard, too. Talent never is enough by itself. It can get one a lucky break and a fast start, but only through intelligence and hard work can the best performers reach the top and stay there.

Professional sports is a talent field that can be extremely profitable, many times more so than in the past. And like pop music, professional sports open the doors of opportunity to everyone with talent. A huge proportion of men and women making fortunes out of baseball, football, basketball, tennis and golf come from impoverished backgrounds, and many are black.

Sports seem to offer real opportunities only to the performers, for, except for those of the National Football League, not a great many franchises make money. For the investors the chief opportunity they afford is the pleasure of frittering away large sums to inflate the spenders' ego.

People also told me that there are many bigger opportunities today than in the past in the practice of law, medicine, accounting and some academic disciplines. There are even big opportunities in some kinds of engineering. The opportunities in these fields are spread all across the land. Almost everyone I talked with was acquainted with someone—perhaps several persons—from his or her own community who had gotten rich in one of these activities.

They also knew that there are few countries where this can happen, and that in most of the foreign free enterprise countries the talented performer, composer, writer or director is likely ultimately to emigrate to the United States in order to achieve full potential.

In the communist and socialist countries opportunities are strictly limited by the law and social structure. In Marxist countries, all talented persons, like all other professionals, even business and management professionals, must become employees of the government, which screens them out of the masses very early in life and gives them special training. They get good salaries (by Socialist standards) and lots of perquisites and privileges as compared with other workers, but they cannot hope to become independent or to accumulate any significant amount to leave to their children. That kind of opportunity is immoral and anti-social, according to the basic Marxist dogma: "from each according to his abilities, to each according to his needs."

Even though they interpret "needs" somewhat liberally, the Communists believe in a leveling process in society, and "wants" count for little. One of the chief reasons they believe the state should own the means of production is so that industry cannot be diverted from satisfying needs to satisfying wants. They charge that in capitalist society most fortunes are made doing just that.

Many American labor union leaders also believe in a leveling process in society, at least in theory. But that doesn't stop a fair number of union leaders from getting rich by means of bribes, kickbacks, frauds, embezzlements, intimidation and political shenanigans.

Some persons told me during my travels that opportunities are increasing because the power of the union leaders, which grew so enormously between 1934 and the early 1970s, now is being curbed. Many said putting restraints on the unions will give small- and middle-sized businesses a better chance to compete and survive.

I personally feel that the union bosses had become much too powerful. Straight economic forces began to curb this power in the mid-1970s, and President Reagan's firm action in the air traffic controllers' strike accelerated it. I also have observed that, when persisted in stubbornly, the unions' advocacy of the leveling process backfires and destroys union jobs. Employers go broke or they move out of the strongly unionized areas into new areas where the labor market is more favorable.

The leveling philosophy inevitably gets in the way of technological progress or businesses' ability to adjust their operations to their true production capabilities and marketing opportunities. The leveling philosophy often causes the union leaders to negotiate for preserving the jobs of all the existing workers instead of for better wages and conditions for those who really are needed. Ultimately, this leads to an explosion or to a collapse. There's a dramatic example of this going on in Britain as this is being written. For years, the printing trades unions in London have refused to accept any technological advances or any reduction whatsoever in the grossly swollen working forces. Suddenly, in the past year, the newspaper and periodical industry moved out of London to new suburban plants employing modern, advanced technology. Thousands of printing workers were fired in London while workers in the new suburban plants received higher wages and better fringe benefits.

The armed forces, with their liberal education and training programs, also afford lots of opportunities. This is something new in our history. As recently as the mid-1930s our Army comprised only 100,000 men, and officer promotion was painfully slow. It was even worse in earlier times. When Teddy Roosevelt was president, he bemoaned the fact that there were so many gray-haired lieutenants in our tiny army.

But the folks I have been talking with around the country said there are plenty of opportunities in the armed forces now. Promotion is fairly rapid for officers and noncoms and the special education and training programs enables many who retire after twenty years in uniform to find excellent civilian jobs or to set up in business for themselves.

The quality of the defense our armed forces are presently capable of providing is quite another story, however.

Selling is still rich in opportunities. Lots of people told me something I have always believed, that if you can sell you can do well in any business; if you can sell one line of products or services, you probably can sell many others. In fact, for the past hundred and fifty years, selling was considered to provide the most opportunities of any field of endeavor in the United States. During many periods in that time, dynamic salesmen have completely dominated industry and commerce. More companies, particularly in manufacturing, distributing, retailing, insurance and marketing of securities, were headed by salesmen than by production or financial executives. Land development companies also usually were headed by high pressure salesmen.

There has been a change in recent years. Men with financial rather than sales training and expertise are most frequently being chosen as chief executive officers.

I have repeatedly noticed during my travels that part-time work is growing astonishingly all across the country. Many businesses depend almost entirely on part-time workers for all sorts of jobs. Married women particularly like part-time jobs because they enable them to spend more time with their husbands and children. They feel safer about the kids than they would if working at a full-time job.

I think the spread of part-time work is good for the nation for many reasons. It gives employers considerably more flexibility in labor management. It enables millions of persons who otherwise would be cooped up doing housework or tied down to boring, routine full-time jobs to get out and meet many people and to gain a wide variety of experience and skills and a generally broader view of business and society than their forebears could have hoped to enjoy.

This makes for happier workers who are more interested in what they are doing. It also improves the motivation for management people. The spread of part-time work helps open the eyes of millions to opportunities for self-improvement and gives them the aspiration for better jobs.

In short, part-time work expands people's vocational, personal, educational and social horizons tremendously.

It is no accident that so many big companies are headed by financial executives with very special education and training nowadays. Many people told me they hoped their kids would get this kind of training.

Finance today is so vastly more complicated than it was in the days when the Morgans and Vanderbilts were in full sway that even an apparently minor mistake in a financial decision can be disastrous. Therefore, decisions always are made with the aid of the electronic computer and a huge amount of available data, analyzed by means of very sophisticated software. A top executive who can sit for some hours in front of a computer terminal and analyze and resolve very complex problems rapidly has a huge advantage. If he isn't a wizard at the cathode screen himself, the top executive must know how to choose assistants who are, and how to evaluate correctly their work. Apparently that doesn't always happen, judging by some of the horrendous financial and policy mistakes made in recent years by some of our biggest corporations and government departments.

I found that very "ordinary" people are quite aware of most of this. Some people said with a knowing smile, "A lot of these big shots don't know anywhere near as much about using the computer as they pretend to."

There should be a lot of opportunities in investment and commercial banking and securities brokerage. Certainly, there is much room for improvement in these fields. I spoke in Chapter 1 about the anger many Americans feel because our big banks have loaned so many billions of dollars without security to foreign countries in order to reap fantastic interest revenues. Many of these loans are perilously close to being defaulted.

Well, Senator Bill Bradley (D-New Jersey) recently added a lot of fuel to this fire in a speech to the National Press Club. He said that the debt crises in Latin America created by these huge loans, some of which were practically forced on the Latins by the American and international banks, have played a big role in causing our huge foreign trade deficit.

Bradley, who advocates cancelling part of Latin America's $350 billion debt to the banks, cutting interest rates sharply on the rest and letting the banks' executives and stockholders lump it, said that because of the vast amounts of interest they have to pay on these loans, the Latinos simply have stopped buying all the things they used to buy from us. That has slashed our exports tremendously. Also, Bradley said, they are so desperate to get cash to pay the interest they dump vast amounts of their own exports on the U.S. markets—textiles, garments, farm products and raw materials for the main part—at very low prices.

Bradley said the loss of exports from Latin America and the dumping of cheap Latin imports had cost at least 1.4 million jobs in the United States.

Again, it is to be hoped that this sad experience will teach our big bankers a lesson and make them more willing to pour their funds into the domestic loan market. They won't get such fantastic interest rates but they will have a lot better security and will have the satisfaction of creating jobs for Americans.

There are still many opportunities in advertising, publishing, radio and motion pictures, if not so many as in the recent past.

There also are opportunities in many service businesses providing various kinds of care for homeowners and commercial establishments. In some of these operations, one can get more equipment and advertising and financial support by acquiring a franchise than is possible on his own. The variety of these opportunities is astonishing and one should survey the field carefully before jumping off the dock.

There still are opportunities in agriculture. Many people do well by growing and packing natural foods and selling them by mail or through nature stores and health food stores.

All of these operations require hard work and above all the courage "to jump off the dock and start swimming."

One important reason America still is the land of opportunity is that our national economy is made up of a number of regional economies, and only once in our history have all these regions suffered at once in a depression or recession. Even in the Great Depression of the 1930s the South did not suffer nearly so severely as the rest of the country.

Also, our economy is so diversified that some industries and vocations prosper and expand steadily even in quite hard times and new industries and trades spring up.

Most importantly, our regional economies tend to be cyclical; bust periods follow boom periods and generally after a decade or so there is a sharp rebound. New England is an example. Things are booming Down East today with new high technology industries, many of them in defense services or products, others in commercial or homeowners' electronics. Securities and financial businesses are thriving in New England. Associated Press Columnist John Cunniff recently wrote that New England "is a hothouse of new ventures."

Yet, New England was on the skids for half a century, starting just before World War I. Its once mighty textile, shoe and machinery manufacturing industries moved away to greener pastures where labor was cheaper. Its great Atlantic Ocean fisheries were sadly depleted and its big lumber trade was only a ghost of what it was in the nineteenth century. The region was living off banking, insurance, book publishing and tourism.

Cunniff noted that all the Atlantic coastal states are doing well now and the eastern half of the midwest is staging a comeback like New England, but after a much shorter period of decline.

This cyclical nature of the regional economies creates all sorts of opportunities—large ventures for the big investors and small local ventures to serve consumers. It also creates real estate booms that make a lot of money for land and home owners, developers and real estate dealers. However, if runaway speculation sets in, sooner or later there will be a painful collapse. But should a family that pays $400,000 for a house that was on sale for $100,000 only four years earlier be surprised or deserve a lot of sympathy if the deal goes sour?

Here is another example of the cyclical nature of our regional economies: For many decades sheep ranching was on the decline in America. Most Americans always did prefer other meats over lamb and mutton and the American sheep rancher had to compete with frozen lamb from Australia and New Zealand. So the American sheep rancher was mainly dependent on his wool clip for a profit. The development of so many modestly priced, durable, flexible and easily laundered synthetic fabrics nearly destroyed the wool market after 1945.

But now wool is coming back into favor for better garments for both males and females and the extremely high current prices for beef are causing housewives to pick up a lot of lamb at the supermarket. So, suddenly there are some new opportunities for sheep ranchers in our western states.

Opportunities like these can only be taken advantage of by free people who are not tied to the land they were born on or subject to being herded about like cattle at the whim of authoritarian governments.

In Chapter 2, I alluded to the enormous number of people all over the world who are eager to come to America, many of whom will risk their lives to get here. To most of these people, opportunity does not mean a chance to get rich quick, it means a start, probably a very humble start. To many of these immigrants, a job as a dishwasher in a restaurant, or a field hand on a farm, a messenger or a day laborer is a real opportunity because it's a start in life, and a start was not possible where they come from. A high percentage of these persons will take full advantage of such a start and will climb the ladder to various degrees of success; some will climb rapidly, some very slowly, but most will climb.

Unhappily, a significant portion of the immigrants, chiefly the illegal ones, see the marketing of marijuana, cocaine and herion and some other criminal activities as their opportunities in America.

What all I have been saying leads up to is that an enormous number of Americans today are millionaires. Inflation is partly responsible and some have become rich by winning on lottery tickets, but most have done so by hard work and by overcoming the various things that are wrong with our economies. Even after the collapse of the oil market whittled down to size some Texas billionaires and multimillionaires (Clint Murchison's net worth is reported to have shrunk from $350 million to $3 million), the number of millionaires in the country keeps growing amazingly. Newspapers and magazines contain stories about new ones everyday.

There are so many nobody can remember their names. They will never be famous the way the Vanderbilts, the Morgans and the Rockerfellers have been famous. In fact, today even a multimillionaire probably will have to hire an expensive press agent to get his name in the papers or on the air.

Just recently newspapers have been publishing new lists of top executives with the biggest annual incomes, those over or approaching $1 million. People I discussed the matter with were amazed and incredulous. "Who are these characters?" they asked. "I never heard of three-fourths of them and may never hear of them again."

But for sure, the opportunities in our land of plenty are so numerous and so varied that we are and probably will be forever the envy of the whole world. One need but apply the old-fashioned four-letter word *work*, and the degree of success will depend on you.

All across our great land of opportunity I found people gearing themselves for unconditional achievement and success, and most of them were delighted with the economic progress of our country during the Reagan years.

CHAPTER 5

# *Keeping Our Population Balance*

THE UNITED STATES is the only large advanced country in the world that has succeeded in preserving an adequate balance of population and home grown food supplies—without exporting people.

Not only have we not had to export people, as all the European nations have, but we have accepted millions of immigrants from all over the world and are still doing so.

For a hundred and fifty years it was extremely easy to maintain the population/food balance because we had so much new land in the west and in some parts of the south and east.

As the fertile new lands filled up with settlers, the great agricultural takeoff that began during World War I enabled us to easily offset the big population increases and still have large surpluses of foodstuffs to sell to the rest of the world.

Curiously, although the agricultural takeoff lasted more than fifty years, a surprising number of Americans never heard of it and don't understand its importance to our

69

economy and the economy of the world. This takeoff was for several decades unique to the United States. It caused the harvests of grain, dairy products, eggs and poultry, meats and fruits and vegetable and feed and forage crops per acre and per manhour of labor to soar suddenly beyond anything mankind ever had dreamed of before.

The crop yields didn't increase slowly, they doubled, tripled and quadrupled within a few years, almost overnight by historical reckoning. This takeoff enabled us to feed most of mankind during both World Wars and for more than a decade following World War II.

The American agricultural takeoff now has been largely duplicated in Europe and in Canada, Australia and New Zealand. The Soviet Union appeared to be achieving such a takeoff in the 1960s, but ran into severe crop failures caused by bad weather and some bad management in the 1970s.

An agricultural takeoff is not just a new phenomenon, it is an extremely complicated one, and the American takeoff could not be duplicated rapidly even by the most advanced countries. That's because it is not just a matter of better seeds, more and better fertilizers, and more machines instead of horses, bullocks and hand labor. A takeoff must be the culmination of years of scientific study and experimentation and drastic changes in popular and official attitudes. It depends most of all on good popular education, on the building by government of vast irrigation and flood control projects, on making electric power and diesel motor fuel available to all farmers, on building vast networks of highways, penetrating even the remotest rural areas, and sophisticated distribution systems involving trains, trucks and aircraft, many of them refrigerated, plus refrigerated warehouses and market halls and huge machine-operated grain elevators and storage towers.

It also depends on new, highly advanced farm banking and crop financing. And it depends on a populace sophisticated enough to take advantage of all these things.

We are presently in the middle of another politically created "farm crisis" growing out of a speculative boom and bust cycle. We have a huge glut of grains and some other crops produced under high government price supports. These crops are salable abroad but unless the federal government subsidizes the exports, the farmers stand to be stuck with them or to take losses on the sales.

This mess is expected to cost American taxpayers $35 billion in 1986 and all that pouring out of taxpayers' money is doing nothing to resolve the crisis, it is only postponing the day of reckoning and foreclosure on their lands for some millions of western farmers who got into the mess by speculation. The only thing the $35 billion outlay will solve is the election year panic of senators and congressmen from the farm states. It undoubtedly will make our farm problem and the world agricultural problem worse.

This $35 billion outlay on price supports and export subsidies contrasts with an average farm support cost of under $5 billion a year during the Carter administration and the first two years President Reagan was in office.

It must be pointed out forcibly that Mr. Reagan is not to blame. The *Newark Star-Ledger* said in an editorial in late July, 1986, that "Congress conceived, ballyhooed and enacted this multi-billion-dollar fiasco without help or encouragement from the Reagan administration. Implementation of the massive giveaway was then thrust upon a reluctant Department of Agriculture. Congress now has an obligation to undertake an immediate review of the costly mischief it has wrought and undo the damage.

The editorial also said any benefits of the vast program "to the small, struggling farmer are yet to appear."

In an article in *The New York Times* late in July, 1986, Michael Fribourg, chairman of Continental Grain Company, said, "Agriculture is in a state of crisis, both nationally and globally, not because of changes in weather, technology or eating habits, but as the result of misguided actions over the past forty years by governments around the world."

Fribourg said these misguided actions and policies have caused the scandals of "food rotting in European warehouses while children starve in Ethiopia, and small farmers being foreclosed in South Dakota while their larger neighbors enjoy increased government subsidies" and of "American farm exports declining even as farm export subsidies are increased."

He said the only solution is to gradually reduce and ultimately stop all price supports and subsidies, and that would have to be accomplished by international cooperation.

How bad off are the farmers and are they really entitled to be bailed out again at the taxpayers' expense?

Well, we can say right off that the farmers' troubles today are not the result of worldwide depression as was the case when President Roosevelt got the first farm price support law enacted in 1933. On July 21, 1986, a reporter for *The New York Times*, William Robbins, wrote, after a trip through the grain belt: "The farm economy's current problems are largely a result of a roller-coaster sort of ride that began in the early 1970s."

Robbins went on to tell how the Soviet crop failures of 1972, the devaluation of the dollar that year and worldwide crop shortfalls in 1974 set off a great wave of speculation in farmland in the United States grain belt. Farmers expanded their operations, expecting to get rich in a hurry through government sponsored grain exports at high prices.

But starting in 1982, the whole business collapsed. Prices of good farmland that had been driven up to $2,000 or $2,500 an acre by speculation and expansion, tumbled slowly until they average about $900 today. The farmers are stuck with mortgages on much of the land based on the inflated prices they paid for it, and much of it is assessed for taxes at the inflated prices.

Prices of grains and other crops fell in much the same ratio.

Banks began foreclosing on the loans taken out to finance the expansion and speculation.

Farmers who did not speculate were hit by the wide fluctuation in crop prices and by increases in taxes on their land as greedy politicians raised tax assessments to approach the inflated market value of adjacent farmland.

So, a lot of these farmers who are getting the benefit of this huge government largesse essentially are only business speculators like people who trade in Wall Street, in urban real estate, in commodities or in some kind of risky new business, or overexpand an established business.

All businesses are speculative to some extent. If these farmers, who speculated in land and grain prices with their eyes open, are entitled to be rescued by the government, then isn't any businessman anywhere who makes a mistake and suffers a loss equally entitled to be rescued at the taxpayers' expense?

The argument that farmers are entitled to rescue "because they are the backbone of the nation" is long outworn. If umpteen thousand farmers go broke and lose their land, so what? Other people will buy their lands at more realistic prices and will farm them on a more realistic basis. Even though they are taking many a well deserved beating on the loans they made to finance the unwise expansion and land speculation, the banks will lend money to the newcomers. They must lend money or go out of business.

As a matter of fact, I discovered that bankers, real estate brokers and insurance company loan officers and agents are more responsible for the farm tragedy than the farmers. They seduced the farmers into taking out the excessive loans and overlarge mortgages and speculating in farm land.

Farmer Bill Jones was urged to buy that "nice tract adjoining your acreage" even though the price seemed high. The moneylenders offered to finance 100 percent of the price for him and assured him that farmland would continue to rise in market value indefinitely "because land is really scarce and we can't make any more of it."

They offered to refinance his existing mortgage and consolidate it with the mortgage on the new tract, giving Bill Jones a little cash to boot.

Poor Jones, dazzled by the high prices of grain at the time, knew that he was paying an inflated price and a high interest rate, but he didn't realize how high, or how insecure the future of grain and land markets was. He didn't know what a deep hole the friendly bankers, real estate dealers or insurance company loan officials were persuading him to dig for himself and his family.

What motivated the real estate men, bankers and insurance companies to treat Bill Jones that way? Just plain greed and social irresponsibility.

Some of the people I met on my travels reminded me that boom and bust cycles in agriculture have occurred all through history. Cupidity and stupidity are not unique to our generation. But greed and foolishness didn't cause all the farm collapses; drought and other natural disasters caused many of them and often Congress and the state legislatures would provide some relief, but until our era, nobody felt farmers ruined by speculation and their own bad judgment should be bailed out by the government. What's so special about the current generation of farmers?

The only thing that is really special about today's farmers is that they have so many well placed persons like Senator Bob Dole in Congress to put pressure on the White House and get the rest of the nation taxed egregiously to bail out their misguided and unlucky constituents.

I have gone into the current farm crisis rather fully because its dimensions show that we are in no danger of losing our balance of population and adequate home grown food supplies soon.

But for the long term, the outlook is not so rosy. Both this

balance and our present food production and distribution systems are vulnerable to a number of perils. The first of these
perils is excessive population growth. We do not have a runaway or explosive population growth as do so many countries
in Latin America, Asia and Africa, but the growth is enough to
cause real concern.

There are several reasons for the excessive population
growth. The first is that our birthrate is not falling fast
enough. Although reputable and concerned scientists tell us
we should do no more than reproduce ourselves—that is, no
more than two children per couple—people keep on having
three to ten kids. Why do they do it? With the omnipresent
availability of birth control information, contraceptive pills
and devices and abortion, family planning ought to be easy.
Nevertheless, many couples who are well-to-do and apparently sophisticated continue to have many children. They
figure that if we can afford to rear more kids why not have
them? Illiterate and semi-literate people have too many children out of sheer ignorance or, sometimes, to collect higher
welfare allowances.

But the real answer is that so many people read very little
and what they do read is confined to escapist fiction or books
and articles about how to make more money. So they don't
learn about the warnings of the scientists on the peril of too
much population growth. Others have religious convictions
against family planning. The children learn a little about it in
school but it isn't given much emphasis. The militant opposition of the Catholic church and some other elements to
planned parenthood makes sure of that.

A very large number of illegitimate births, a much higher
rate than ever in our past, is nearly as great a cause of excessive population growth as married couples having too many
babies.

I didn't find people on my travels much concerned about
the birth rate aspect of the long-term population problem.

Many of them had not heard of the warnings of the scientists. Others simply were not inclined to heed the warnings. I found people much more concerned about another cause of overpopulation—illegal immigration. They were quite divided on the subject, but everybody had an opinion. The majority were quite indignant about the hordes of illegals pouring into the country over the Mexican and Canadian borders and through our many international airports with forged passports and visas. Many more simply arrive on tourist visas and never go home again.

But others I talked with said illegal immigrants are necessary as a source of labor for agriculture and small businesses, particularly small manufacturers. They said the illegal immigrants fill many necessary menial jobs that are spurned by native Americans. That certainly is true in affluent times, but it wouldn't be true during a depression or a really severe recession; then the native Americans would be glad to get the menial jobs.

Congress, the White House and the federal bureaucracy are under tremendous pressure from Latin American immigrants and their immediate descendants, and even from Latin American governments, to go easy on the flood of illegals coming from Latin America and to grant amnesty to the Latin illegals who have been here a number of years.

No one really knows how many illegal immigrants are living in the country. The U.S. Immigration and Naturalization Service makes estimates but cannot verify them. One reason is that a lot of the illegals come and go. They stay a few months or a couple of years, make a stake and return to their homeland to spend it, then make their way back to the United States unlawfully to make a new stake.

This is particularly true of the criminal element of the illegals, including the dealers in marijuana, cocaine and heroin.

The Immigration and Naturalization Service catches a lot of the "wetbacks" crossing our southern border from Mexico and sends them back. But those who get sent back try again in a few days, a few weeks or a few months. Finally they succeed in crossing the border and reaching relatives or friends in one of our cities.

Stopping the flood of illegals who arrive by airliner with forged documents is an impossible task for the INS with its small staff and budget. In the days before the cheap international airline fare it was easier. Then the INS had to watch only the port cities. An incoming ship could be boarded, sealed and searched thoroughly. Also, a steamship fare was much higher in relation to the economics of the times than airline fare is today, so fewer illegal aliens could afford trying to get in that way.

Many illegal aliens have little fear of being deported. They know if they are caught, deportation proceedings can be dragged out for a couple of years if they have a smart lawyer, and they may eventually win a court order allowing them to stay in the United States. Recently, the New York police and federal narcotics agents have been complaining bitterly that the INS will not try to carry out deportation orders issued by the courts against illegal aliens convicted of drug offenses. The officers say many of these aliens who have been ordered deported by a judge are picked up on another offense within a few weeks and sometimes are picked up for a third or fourth offense long after they were supposed to have been sent back to their homelands.

Again, the INS officials say they simply don't have the staff and budget to cope with the situation.

There is no question that illegal immigration is causing overpopulation just as open and free immigration began to increase the population alarmingly after World War I, resulting in the enactment of our first immigration control law, which went in effect in 1924.

The fact that we imported more agricultural products in 1986 then we exported is no threat to our population/food supply balance. What are these imports? Fine wines and many kinds of exotic and gourmet foods for the most part. They satisfy our wants, not our needs, and we can stop buying them anytime we please. On the other hand, the farm products we export tend to be basic crops—grains, cotton, meats, dairy products, citrus fruits and some other fruits and vegetables. They satisfy people's needs.

However, in the long term, our balance of population and home grown foods is vulnerable to several perils and we already have lost a lot in terms of the quality of our national diet.

A close friend of mine who lives in New Jersey says Jersey no longer has any real right to call itself the Garden State. That name is a cruel hoax. Only twenty years ago, he says, New Jersey grew more than half its own food; today 80 percent of it is imported from other states and foreign countries. No longer can you find Jersey strawberries, peaches, apples, corn, tomatoes and green vegetables all summer in abundance in the supermarkets. No longer are the state's highways dotted in summer and fall with farmers' stands selling fresh high quality home grown fruits and vegetables.

About twenty thousand acres of farmland are taken out of production in New Jersey every year. The number of farmers in the state has dropped from twenty thousand to nine thousand since 1950.

What has happened in New Jersey has happened in many other states.

Produce grown by local market gardeners and small farmers tends to be more flavorful and can be more nearly ripe when it is offered for sale than the mass produced fruits and vegetables grown on huge overspecialized ranch-type farms and shipped across the country or from Mexico.

These huge farms have to be extremely specialized in selecting crops to plant. They cannot afford to grow anything for which the demand is less than enormous. Therefore many good things that were offered for sale every day in season in the days when local market farmers supplied the grocery stores through local wholesalers are no longer to be had. When was the last time you saw gooseberries, black raspberries, persimmons, mustard greens or up to five varieties of fresh beans on your supermarket shelves?

Even the varieties of canned and frozen fruits and vegetables are reduced by this overspecialization of agriculture on the big ranch-type farms.

The quality of American life definitely has suffered from this overconcentration and overspecialization in agriculture.

One has to suspect that many of these overspecialized corporate farm ventures mainly exist only to collect vast federal price support funds on basic crops and are not much interested in servicing the public.

But there are other aspects of our new overspecialized, overconcentrated agricultural system that pose perils to our balance of population and food supply. The huge farms, of course, are vulnerable like smaller farms to drought (although some of them have very costly and effective irrigation systems), other natural disasters and plain bad weather. On the whole, the new system may be more vulnerable to natural disasters than the older system of local market production.

It is also more vulnerable to trucking strikes and farm laborers' strikes. It seems irrelevant in view of the present glut of petroleum, but the big farms are very vulnerable to petroleum and energy shortages like the one the Arab nations created in the 1970s.

What has caused the decline of the local market gardener and small local commercial farmer is not inability to compete. The supermarkets are quite willing to buy their crops when they are available. No, the cause is the buying up of the rich garden and farmland by real estate developers in order to build luxury and semi-luxury housing, shopping centers and industrial park centers. The farmers sold out because they were offered tremendous prices for the land and they could quit work and retire to Florida or Arizona.

Some of the local farmers were actually forced out of business because their land was rezoned and the tax assessments raised sharply. This ought to be illegal. Agricultural land, wherever it is, is supposed to be assessed for taxes only on the basis of the income it can earn by agriculture. The high values of adjacent residential or commercial property should never be allowed to influence the assessment of agricultural land for tax purposes.

However, the local farmers who are forced off their lands also get very high prices from the developers, so they rarely complain, they just take the money and head for retirement areas where the climate and the fishing are good or are supposed to be.

However, this situation raises the possibility that at some time in the not remote future, Congress and the state legislatures will have to consider forbidding the diversion of any more farmland to residential, commercial or industrial use.

For many decades, our surpluses of food in the face of an ever-growing population brought us great prestige and power in the world. But while a healthy surplus is seen to be the result of wisdom and strength, a subsidized glut such as we have now is viewed by the rest of the world as evidence of folly and weakness on our part.

Every time we raise farm price supports, other food exporting nations take advantage of it by increasing their output of these same crops and underselling us in the international markets. So the price supports, export subsidies, import quotas and other distortions of farm trade simply aggravate the problems they are supposed to solve. The only real solution is to whittle them all away.

The best thing to do with overlarge crop carryovers, as surpluses used to be called, would be to use them to alleviate hunger in the impoverished countries of the world. Governments still would have to pay the farmers for food dispensed that way or make money grants to the impoverished countries so they could buy the grains and other foodstuffs in the regular markets. But that would be a lot simpler and would make more sense than export subsidies for ever-growing farm price supports.

To whittle down the farm price supports and stop export subsidies we would have to get the cooperation of the other food exporting nations, and to do that we would first have to take bold and realistic steps towards cleaning our own house. That would require having men and women in Congress with the instincts of statesmen—the instinct to face up to hard reality and put the welfare of the whole nation always ahead of the immediate needs and desires of their own constituents. In short, we need Senators and Congressmen who put principles ahead of getting re-elected.

It was the cowardly professional politicians, whose only real concern in life is to get re-elected at any cost and any sacrifice of principle and wisdom, who listened to the scared farmers and then persuaded a reluctant President Reagan to subsidize new wheat sales to the Soviet Union. Soon Soviet leaders and Russian housewives will be chortling because they can buy bread from American wheat for much less than Americans must pay.

The president approved the subsidy much against the advice and wishes of State Department officials. They warned him that the subsidy on wheat sales to the Russians can only infuriate other food exporting nations and cause them to retaliate against us, thus aggravating the global agricultural overproduction crisis and lowering the prestige of the United States throughout the world.

Ironically, the Russians refused to buy the American wheat even at the subsidized prices because other countries offered them wheat at even cheaper prices.

We don't need that kind of folly to keep our population and home-grown food supply in balance.

CHAPTER 6

# Can Tax Reform Help?

IT WILL take two or three years to tell whether or not the Tax Reform Act of 1986 really will help the economy of the United States.

The new law is not a tax cut *per se*, although it will take about six million low-income persons off the tax rolls and will reduce taxes for many others. It's not a cosmetic job either; it makes some real and formidable changes in the way businesses are taxed by repealing many tax credits and allowances. This will compel some major changes in business strategies.

But it is not a revolution. The law does not attack some of the major evils of the present system.

One big defect is that it ignores the problem of the untaxed underground economy which, according to a number of experts, amounts to up to 30 percent of the total economy.* The people involved are businessmen and workers who handle all their transactions "under the table" and criminals who pay lit-

---

*See *A Nation Saved*, by Arthur Milton, Citadel Press, Secaucus, N.J., 1983.

tle or no federal taxes and cheat a lot on state and local sales taxes.

The new law assumes, like the old law, that the IRS and the Department of Justice will compel all people to pay income, Social Security and excise taxes. It's a stupid assumption. Effective enforcement will have to depend on some new method of attacking the underground economy, on a tax that cannot be evaded.

Those who drafted the new tax law clearly made no attempt to discover such a method. Admittedly, it would be a difficult task. Much sterner punishments for tax evasion probably would be required and, since many of the persons in the underground economy, including illegal aliens, are near the bottom of the social and economic scales, Congress is reluctant to go after them. The reluctance doesn't make much political sense because most of the people in the underground economy probably do not vote. They don't want to call their existence to the attention of the authorities by registering.

The loudest trumpeting about the new law is that it transfers $120 billion in income taxes from individuals to corporations, over the next five years. Incidentally a lot of reporters and commentators leave out that "over the next five years" and inadvertantly make it appear that business will be socked an extra $120 billion a year, an absurdity.

But conservative commentator William Buckley says the transfer ultimately will prove to be a sham because "corporations don't pay taxes, they pass those along to consumers." If Buckley is right, and he often is, that means the $120 billion can't really be transferred to business but will be paid by the same people who have been paying all the taxes for years—the individual consumers.

There is a way to test the logic of Buckley's contention. A corporation is an artificial entity. It has no life or existence except through its stockholders and customers. Therefore the only way it can get money to pay taxes is to take it either from the stockholders or from the customers, and management can be counted on to see to it that the money comes from the customers. Did you ever hear of a corporation's board of directors assessing shareholders to pay the company's tax?

Of course, it can be argued that the stockholders are paying the tax because it reduces the amount of net profit available to pay their dividends and reduces the growth in value prospects of their shares. But this argument doesn't really hold water. The customers still are the sole source of the money that pays the income tax and the dividends. They pay the income tax because it is factored into the company's pricing basis.

Buckley's contention should open a big can of worms for Congress and for economists. A lot of people, including Senator William Proxmire of Wisconsin, have contended for years that taxing corporations on their profitability is fundamentally wrong because it penalizes the honest and efficient corporations by taxing their net income heavily and rewards inefficient and dishonest corporation managements by letting them get off without paying a penny to the government in income tax.

On that score, the Citizens for Tax Justice Committee published a report in July, 1986, saying that more than half of the country's largest corporations have avoided paying any income tax in at least one of the past five years. The committee said one giant, which had $25 billion in operating profit between 1982 and 1985, did not pay a penny in income taxes during this period because of allowances and credits. Remember that the earnings reports showing profits that corporations release to the financial press do not necessarily jibe with the final reports they file with the IRS.

But these corporations collected the taxes they didn't pay from their customers. If you don't believe that, look up the earnings reports of corporations that report losses in the *Wall Street Journal* or some other big newspaper. Invariably, the accountants report the loss as "after taxes" and a reserve for the taxes not actually paid is shown in the profit and loss statement.

If the expected taxes are factored into the company's pricing basis—and you can be sure they are—then the company that reports a loss is, in effect, embezzling the tax money from its customers and from the government. That's perfectly legal and it conforms to the moral theory of the present tax law and present business morality, but is it fair to either the government or the customers, and does it really make sense?

Obviously, the way to deal with the situation is to repeal the corporate income tax, as Senator Proxmire proposed, and substitute another tax for it. It is a matter of record that when the first income tax law was enacted, most congressmen were dubious about the wisdom of applying it to corporations, that's why the initial corporate rate was set at only 1 percent in 1913.

The only substitute taxes that really would correct the situation have been frequently proposed—a value added tax or a gross receipts tax. Several countries rely on this kind of tax as their primary source of revenue after the individual income tax, or even before the income tax.

Such a levy would tax all corporations equally without regard to whether they are profitable or lose money. But that idea scares hell out of the politicians even though it is clear that it would generate a lot more revenue than our present system. For example, in spite of his harsh criticism of the corporate income tax as being unsound in principle and unfair in operation, Senator Proxmire always opposed the idea of a value added tax, saying it would be regressive.

But if Bill Buckley is right, switching from the corporate tax to a value added or gross receipts tax couldn't be regressive because it wouldn't change the source of the money—the consumers who pay all taxes. It could only be regressive in the minds of the uninformed and the politicians who cater to the uninformed to get elected and re-elected.

The 20 percent alternative minimum tax on corporation earnings provided for in the new law is designed to correct the abuses of credits and allowances, and offset the ingenuity of management executives and accountants in putting them together legally.

Only a value added or gross receipts tax could get at the revenues of these companies, who, like companies that have a profit, are collecting invisible taxes from their customers—the public—and are not passing the money on to the government.

Most of the federal tax revenues are collected through business and to the average businessman it undoubtedly seems that much of them are paid by business. A large part of the individual income tax and the Social Security tax are collected by withholdings from wages and salaries. Import duties and excise taxes also are collected through business firms.

But the high corporate income tax on profitability gives management a chance to wrest money from the government by various shenanigans and errors. It has distorted managerial policies ever since it became a permanent feature of our society during the Great Depression.

The first high corporate income tax occurred during World War I and was frankly a war tax. It did not influence mangerial policy significantly. After that war, the corporate income tax rates remained too low to influence managerial policies significantly until the Great Depression. Then the high rates were imposed for a purpose that hardly would be recognized today—to put a stop to excessive retention of earnings by corporations on behalf of those who controlled the companies. If earnings were retained and not paid out in dividends they could not be taxed at the relatively high individual income tax rates, but the retained earnings could be used for a wide variety of purposes that benefited those who controlled the company. Congress put a stop to that by raising the corporate tax rate so management either had to pay the earnings out in dividends or see Uncle Sam grab them. The rates have stayed

high ever since for many reasons—three wars for example—
and the distortions in managerial policy have been magnified
and multiplied.

If there were no corporate income tax, there would be no
"tax dollars" to waste on investment in dubious ventures designed primarily as tax shelters for other income. Extravagant
entertainment and excessive salaries would have to come
right out of operating profit, not partly out of "tax dollars."

This raises a warning note. If we should repeal the corporate income tax, we might have to adopt a tax on excessive
retained corporate earnings and an excess profits tax—a levy
on earnings above a statutorily prescribed rate or return on
investment or percentage of gross income. Otherwise, the
concentration of the power of corporate wealth would hit us
hard again.

The next thing about the new tax law that has been noted
by many skeptical commentators is that it is based on a lot of
assumptions that may prove false. These assumptions involve
future inflation, the future course of employment and
unemployment, the foreign trade deficit and, above all, the
budget deficit. Those who were in a position to observe
closely the drafting of the new law say many of these assumptions may be far too optimistic.

Also, there are many question marks. Nobody knows for
sure what the impact of individual sections of the new law will
be. Will ending the deductibility of credit card interest hit retail sales and travel and entertainment very much? Will the
repeal of the investment tax credit cause higher prices and
worker layoffs as well as a slowdown in new industrial ventures? Will the new restraints on the issuance of tax exempt
bonds by the states and municipalities have a crippling effect
not only on construction but on the expansion of industry?

As with almost everything else, I found people I talked
with terribly divided about the new tax law. The one thing
they agreed on was that it cannot be of any quick help in

reducing the budget deficit; Congress will have to come up with other means of accomplishing that. Also, it was generally agreed that, from now on, people will not be willing to invest in real estate or building primarily as a tax shelter. They will put their money into such a venture only if it can be reasonably expected to earn a profit.

People involved in many social uplift movements like the law, but old-line charitable institutions fear it will cut heavily into their gifts.

Although everybody said the new law will be a help to the working poor, some people observed that it doesn't do anything for the unemployed. Well, it's a little hard to understand how a tax law could do anything for the jobless. Other measures and economic recovery are needed for that.

Restaurant and hotel people naturally were fearful about the impact of slashing deductions for business meals to 80 percent. A curious reaction came from an official of a big motel chain. He said the new law could curb the building of new motels primarily as tax shelters and that should improve the occupancy rates of existing motels and hotels.

Banking people were upset about the new law's provision that takes away from larger banks their deduction for the cost of maintaining bad loan reserves.

On the whole, though, it seems to me that unless one is very directly hurt or benefited by a specific provision of the new law, it will be wise to heed the old adage that "Fools rush in where angels fear to tread" and reserve opinion on the law for a while.

# CHAPTER 7

# Can We Solve Our Insurance Muddles?

P EOPLE BUYING life insurance today have a much
better chance of receiving adequate value for their premium
dollars and real protection for their families than they did only
a few years ago.

But the insurance business as a whole is in sad disarray.
Professional malpractice and product liability coverage are
priced so high they are unaffordable to many who need the
protection. This insurance is no longer available in many parts
of the country. Ordinary automobile and fire insurance costs
have gone up alarmingly in some areas. These muddles can be
solved, but it will take more diligence and more honesty than
is presently being brought to bear on the problems.

For one hundred and fifty years the Establishment life insurance companies have acted as if they had licenses to steal.
They have grossly misinformed the public and the state insurance regulators about the nature of the business and its true
actuarial bases and costs. They have brainwashed armies of

agents into selling vast amounts of overpriced whole life, cash value insurance that afforded families hardly any protection against the hazard of early death of the breadwinner.

Now, in the last quarter of this century, new life companies and armies of new agents and established independent agents are offering families in their prime years adequate financial protection at reasonable prices.

Billions of dollars' worth of new term life insurance has been sold in the last few years, much of it replacing expensive outmoded cash value insurance.

I predict that the sale of cash value life insurance will be effectively outlawed in the United States by the year 2000.

People power, which I talked about in Chapter 1, will force legal outlawing of the costly, inadequate policies or will simply make it impossible to sell them.

Some need may remain for straight whole life insurance without cash values, but I predict the sale of all whole life insurance will fall drastically.

But for now, the term life companies, their agents and the independent agents have a long way to go to replace most of the nearly $3 trillion of over-priced cash value, whole life policies presently in force.

One big reason for that is that the predatory Establishment companies, fighting grimly to retain their privileges and power and their ill-gotten gains, have persuaded the state regulatory authorities to issue complicated rules controlling the replacement of existing life policies. These rules require expensive and time-consuming paper work on the part of the agent selling the term replacement policies. It is possible for an agent to comply with these regulations and sell term life policies replacing costly, inadequate old policies if the agent is studious and persistent, but it's very difficult.

These anti-replacement rules were originally proclaimed ostensibly to curb wasteful over-competition and to prevent unscrupulous agents from shifting policies with no real benefit to the consumer just to generate new commissions. But, in practice, the rules have served mainly to keep in force billions of dollars of high cost inadequate insurance and thus rob policyholders of substantial parts of their income. These policies have been sold on the basis of misinformation and some outright chicanery.

The proper solution to this problem is federal regulation of the entire insurance industry—life, liability and property/casualty. One national regulatory authority should be cheaper to operate than fifty state authorities, and we would have uniform regulations all across the land. A single powerful federal agency should be a lot more concerned with consumers' rights and needs than fifty state agencies subject to local political influence and lobbying.

Under state regulation, the life insurance industry is exempt from the federal anti-trust laws. This doctrine was reaffirmed in the McCarran-Ferguson Act passed in 1945. When the Federal Trade Commission began its study of the life insurance business in the late 1970s and presented its devastating report in 1979, the companies tried to get an amendment passed to the act that created the FTC that would forbid it from even investigating life insurance. But President Carter upheld the FTC and blocked the amendment.

But in May, 1980, the FTC suffered a setback in its efforts to bring about insurance reform when the Senate and House conferees put severe limits on the commission's ability to investigate the industry. As a result, the FTC now can conduct an investigation of the insurance business only if requested to do so by either the Senate or House Commerce Committees.

I believe that, in addition to federal regulation, we need a self-regulatory national body representing the dealers in all kinds of insurance and perhaps the allied field of financial planning.

Also, I sometimes think that just as the cigarette manufacturers are required to put a label on every pack carrying the surgeon-general's warning that smoking can be dangerous to your health, the marketers of cash value life insurance should be required to put labels on their policies saying that cash value life insurance may prove dangerous to your financial health.

Inflation had quite a lot to do with the revolution that is going on now in life insurance. Inflation heavily emphasized the glaring deficiencies of whole life, cash value insurance. If one took out a $10,000 or a $25,000 policy thirty years ago, that seemed like a tidy sum, but by the late 1970s the purchasing power of such sums had been whittled down by inflation until they seemed ridiculous in terms of financial protection for a widow. Many of the people I talked with on my travels said inflation awakened them to the fact that whole life, cash value policies they bought so proudly and had been paying on for years were of very little value and probably were very near to outright swindles to begin with.

The only legitimate purpose of life insurance is to protect the family against the great hazard of early death of the breadwinner. We need life insurance protection against the peril of early death only during our prime years, and during these years we need the greatest amount of protection possible for the smallest possible premium payments.

In writing the policy, the insurance company is making a wager that the insured will not die while the policy is in force. Therefore, the shorter the term of the policy and the longer the odds the insurance company can give, the more protection it can offer for the least money.

That's how term life insurance works. Of course, as the insured grows older and the policy is renewed annually or after a period of years, the odds shorten and either the premium goes up or less insurance protection is provided. In practice, the premium payments and the amount of protection can be averaged out and levelled over periods of, say, twenty years, and this is done by some companies who are interested in giving the consumer a break.

But for a hundred and fifty years, the Establishment life companies have sold their policies as financial protection against ultimate death, which is not a hazard but a certainty, for we all must die. The overwhelming majority of persons do not need financial protection against ultimate death. By the time they die, their obligations to their children will have been discharged. There are, of course, a few exceptions where life insurance may be needed after the family is grown. Those with handicapped dependents, others that may still need a small policy to assure themselves of a decent burial because they have no other assets, or special business arrangements or sometime tax obligations that must be covered. High cost cash value insurance is not the answer even here. Why not low cost term insurance till age 100 without cash build-up and without any frills? Pure death insurance at the right price can be a blessing under such circumstances.

The insurance company also is making a wager when it sells a whole life policy. It is betting that the insured will not die young but will live to a ripe old age with the company collecting fat annual premiums on his or her policy. The insurance company also is making another wager that the average policyholder doesn't know about or realize. The company is betting that the policy will lapse or be cancelled and the death benefit never will have to be paid. The odds are overwhelmingly in favor of the company on this wager. A very high proportion of whole life policies do lapse—23 percent in the first year and a half or two after they are issued, and they continue to lapse or be cancelled at a slower but steady rate.

These lapses should lengthen the odds in favor of the policyholders, but they don't. The odds to the policyholders on whole life and especially whole life, cash value insurance policies remain very short.

The big thing is that unless we are quite rich nearly all of us need life insurance financial protection during our prime years, and the only way we can get it is through term life insurance. Whole life, cash value insurance is a snare and a delusion.

With a good term life policy, a young man who is earning only $20,000 a year can leave his wife and children $150,000 or even $250,000 if he dies. For persons in their sixties and seventies the cost of such protection by means of term life insurance is extravagant or even prohibitive. The money to pay the very high premiums can be better invested in other ways.

For many years, the Establishment life insurance companies further shortened the odds in their favor and against the policyholders in other ways. They consistently based their premium rates on outmoded mortality tables that lagged far behind the actual mortality experience of the public and made the insurance companies' risks appear to be bigger than they actually were. They refused to write insurance for women, for black people and for persons with only minor physical disabilities, and they grossly exaggerated the perils of many occupations in order to reject their applications or charge them exorbitant premiums.

A large proportion of the over-priced, inadequate whole life policies now in force have been sold on the false theory that insurance is cheaper, a tremendous bargain, if you buy it while you are very young. Of course the premium is low, but you will be paying it for an awful lot of years. The fact is that, in spite of the confusing variety of whole life policies and the astonishing differences in premium rates quoted by various companies for practically identical policies, it is generally true that the overall cost averages out the same, no matter at what age the policy is purchased. All persons have the same average life span. The Establishment company agents will admit this if pressed but keep right on kidding the public that one

At White House reception for "The President's Committee," Spring 1986.

With General Vernon Walters at reception for United
Nations ambassadors at the United States Mission, New
York City.

Receiving award for ten years of programming on Armed
Forces Radio Service ▷

With my wife, Phyllis, and former President Richard
Nixon, New York City, 1986.

With Bill Bresnan on his ABC radio show, discussing the best-seller *How Your Life Insurance Policies Rob You.*

With Ellis Arnall, former governor and attorney-general of the state of Georgia.

With friend and client Guy Lombardo.

Typical of speeches and lectures given across the country.

With Farrah Fawcett.

With the New York Met Rusty Staub.

With Lionel Hampton.

With fellow author Alex Haley and friends.

With actor John Hurt.

With Governor of Oklahoma
George Nigh.

With Jeane Kirkpatrick at United States Mission to the
United Nations.

·should buy life insurance while very young "because it's cheaper."

The fact is that very young single persons do not need life insurance protection except in some special circumstances.

An even worse delusion, which the Establishment company agents do nothing to dispel, is that by purchasing cash value life insurance you can eat your cake and have it too, that the protection doesn't cost much because sooner or later you or your beneficiary will get back virtually every cent you have paid in on the policy. This can happen but it's a rare experience. You generally pay in a lot more than you or your beneficiary get back when the time value of money is figured into the equation.

The lapsing of so many policies ought to be enough to dispel this eat-your-cake-and-have-it-too delusion for anyone who takes the trouble to think about it, but there's another more important truth puncturing the delusion: The accumulated cash values of a life policy are not added to the death benefit.

The Establishment companies for many years have sedulously pushed the idea that life insurance is a good way to save money and a good way to invest. Nothing could be farther from the truth. Any ordinary passbook savings bank account will accumulate savings much faster by virture of its compound interest structure than even the most generous cash value life insurance policy. Insured market rate accounts, certificates of deposit, IRAs, Keogh plans and a considerable variety of other savings instruments that a good financial adviser will find for you will outperform any cash value life insurance policy by a wide margin.

As for being a good investment tool, the 1979 Federal Trade Commission survey report found that, on the average, cash value life insurance yielded a return of only 1.3 percent to policyholders in 1977. The commission said a reasonable return would have been 4 percent and that if that yield had been paid by the companies the policyholders would have received $3.7 billion more.

Well, anyone familiar with the investment business knows that most other types of investments were earning yields much more than 4 percent in 1977 and several times 1.3 percent.

Some sales persons for big Establishment companies selling whole life or universal cash value insurance will boast to you that their companies will be earning 12 to 13 percent annually on investments in the foreseeable future. But how much of that will be passed on to policyholders? As little as possible, you can bet. Most of it will go into added investment and underwriting reserves and big bonuses and salary boosts for the company executives.

The universal life policy, what is it?

No matter what name it goes by it's a gimmick and a sham. It was introduced by the old-line companies when the annual statistical reports showed more than half of the new life insurance being sold was term rather than whole life, cash value. It was ushered in a few years ago with much fanfare by some of the smaller old-line companies and quickly taken up by the giants. Its stated purpose was "to bridge the gap between term and whole life and incorporate the good features of both."

Well, that's plainly impossible on the face of the matter. Universal life policies have a lot of gimmicky options that make them sound very flexible, like giving the policyholder the right to alter the face value of the policy, the premium and some other terms to meet the changing protection needs of their families.

"What's new about that?" I was asked on my travels. "Anybody can buy a new, more suitable life insurance policy and cancel his old policy."

Others I talked with said shrewdly that the universal life

policy looked like a public relations cosmetic job on traditional whole life, cash value insurance, "the same old thing by
a different name."

They are absolutely right. The universal life policy is just a
desperation hoax designed to keep as much of the total business as possible locked up in the hands of the Establishment
companies at the same old high profit margins even though
the new competition has forced the companies to shave those
profit margins a little.

The friends on my travels noticed another gimmick about
the universal life policy. They said it was being sold as a somewhat mysterious sort of status symbol. The policies were being endowed with a mystique to create more demand for
them. Well, the mystique is one of the oldest ideas in the art
of selling and it always has been a favorite tool of con men and
fakers. It has been used in religion, the arts and politics as
well as business.

In essence, the mystique is based on the idea that if something is hard to understand, it must be important and desirable. The universal life insurance policy fits that formula to a
"T," because when the companies got around actually to writing the policy and trying to make them square with the sales
promotion literature, they discovered it just couldn't be done.

So, they settled for making the policies utterly incomprehensible. The executives of the companies can't understand
them, agents in the field can't make sense out of them, and
neither can the editors and writers in the insurance trade
press and general financial press.

And now that ordinary folk are beginning to realize that the
policies are incomprehensible except as disguises for plain
old-fashioned whole life, cash value insurance, I predict the
universal life policy will gradually fade away into limbo.

Life insurance had a very bad reputation in the nineteenth
century. The business was widely and deeply penetrated by
criminals, sharp lawyers and shady businessmen. Many

companies were fly-by-night and a high proportion of the policies written were outright frauds. Death claims were rejected
on the flimsiest of pretexts and claimants, mainly widows,
were stonewalled because they lacked the money to go into
court and sue.

The whole mess was cleaned up almost miraculously in a
single year by a brilliant and determined New York lawyer
named Charles Evans Hughes. He persuaded the legislature
at Albany to adopt the life insurance reform code of 1905,
which quickly became a model for the rest of the country. The
outright criminals and the fly-by-night companies were
driven out of business. Life insurance became respectable
and the industry grew rapidly.

From a distance of eighty years, it would appear that, although Hughes cleaned up the industry and drove out the
criminals and rogues, he never did perceive the basic unfair-
ness of whole life, cash value life insurance and the inherent
corruption of the "respectable" companies. Hughes was an
honorable and energetic man and if he had understood the
full extent of the evil he would have fought it.

The business grew tremendously and because of the vast
capital and reserves it acquired life insurance became an
enormous financial entity with vast power to influence the
economy in both the private and public sectors. The development of group life insurance, health insurance, and later on of
key man jumbo business life insurance and pension underwriting added greatly to the life insurance companies' prow-
ess.

Group life insurance is term insurance, written for the term
of the worker's employment and renewed and expanded periodically as the workers' pay goes up. It is vastly cheaper than
individual whole life, cash value insurance. Inevitably, the
success of group life got some insurance men interested in the
possibility of achieving much the same success by selling term
life insurance on an individual basis. They started out in a

rather modest way and were successful but they soon had to realize that individual term insurance was anathema to the big Establishment companies and they would have a long uphill battle to sell it on a mass basis.

But now, the term life companies have succeeded in grabbing the lion's share of the annual new business. Even the biggest old-line companies have been forced reluctantly to start offering individual term insurance. They offer it only on a restricted basis, however, and discourage their agents from selling it.

In late 1985, the New York State Insurance Commissioner fined, substantially, several life insurance companies for selling group cash value insurance. The reason they gave was that the individuals in the group were not given a fair shake with cash value policies and it was not a good deal for the individuals in the group. If that is the case, how come individual cash value policies sold to individuals is good for them?

You can easily see why, in the not too distant future, cash value policies can become extinct.

Don't let an agent who is biased or subject to big company discipline discourage you from buying term life protection for your family.

The current crisis in liability insurance seems to me to be more the fault of the insurance companies than of the courts, the trial lawyers or the public.

The people I talked with during my travels were very divided on this matter, putting almost equal blame on the companies, the courts and the public.

The courts have contributed to the crisis by coming up with some strange new judicial doctrines that extend and distort traditional law. The public started affairs moving toward the crisis by greedy, infantile behavior, filing many inflated, frivolous and sometimes outrightly fraudulent lawsuits.

But it is the property/casualty and liability insurance companies who should have kept the situation under control and failed to do so. To say the least, they have been extremely neglectful of the interests of their customers and the general public.

The crisis is very real.

Some physicians are being forced to quit practice because they cannot get affordable malpractice insurance. Other professional persons, small businesses and even municipalities have trouble getting liability insurance, and if they can find the coverage the price is likely to be so high they have to boost prices of their service or products, sometimes exorbitantly.

The skyrocketing cost of product liability insurance is making the introduction of new products extremely risky for manufacturers and new products traditionally are the life blood of manufacturing. The manufacturers and marketers also find expensive product liability lawsuits and insurance a heavy burden on established products.

Moral cowardice on the part of judges is in part responsible for this situation. Many of today's judges lack the courage their forebears had and fail to throw out frivolous and unmerited liability suits. They let them go to the jury. This not only runs up huge court costs, it encourages the filing of more frivolous and unmerited suits with resulting damage to the economy.

Rises in the cost of ordinary automobile insurance affect everyone. The introduction of the no-fault concept a few years back has done little to help.

As a result, some millions of persons drive without insurance, most of them illegally—and have many costly accidents that have to be paid for out of the various state uninsured motorist pools. Ironically, the uninsured motorist pools are financed by surcharges on the insurance costs of the insured drivers.

Some time-honored public events have had to be called off because liability insurance could not be obtained at a cost the show or fair's potential revenues could sustain. Schools and some colleges have found the cost of liability coverage for football and basketball games prohibitive or that the insurance costs sop up most of the box office receipts.

Of course, the increasing propensity of the American public to sue at the drop of a hat is a big factor. A damage claim no longer is viewed by many as a matter of seeking fair compensation but is looked on as a lottery ticket that might win a bonanza.

The lawyers who go after jumbo verdicts in these suits look for cases against municipalities, rich corporations and individuals who have large excess liability insurance policies or huge private assets. There's little point in fighting for a million dollar judgment against a chap who has only $50,000 liability insurance and owns nothing except a heavily mortgaged house.

The lawyers generally take the cases on a contingent fee basis; the lawyer will get one-third of whatever he can collect by settlement or trial—plus expenses. The United States is one of the very few countries where this is allowed. In most countries a lawyer can get only his standard per diem fee or an "appropriate" flat fee, plus expenses. He cannot get a percentage of the award. An appropriate flat fee is what the court will allow.

The volume of inflated, frivolous and fraudulent claims has been sufficient to upset the liability insurance rate structure sharply, much more so in malpractice and product and service liability than in personal injury liability. That this volume has affected rates more than it should have is the fault of the insurance companies.

To an increasing extent, the top management of insurance companies is not composed of insurance men but of financiers who are little concerned about insurance operations and the welfare of policyholders or the public. This is particularly apt to be true of insurance companies owned and controlled by conglomerate corporations.

Instead, the top executives indulge in narrow-minded bottom-line thinking and tactics. They look at the prime function of their companies as being to make investments at maximum yields even if the investments sometimes are risky.

Hearings have been held recently in Washington by the Senate Labor and Human Resources Committee on the liability insurance crisis.

Not surprisingly, witnesses for the insurance companies and some lawyers told the senators that the courts are mainly to blame. They said that in the past fifteen years the courts had extended the time before statutes of limitations take effect against tort claims beyond all reasonable bounds, and shifted the burden of proof from the plaintiffs to the doctors in malpractice suits, and had distorted other traditional aspects of the law so as to bring about huge and unwarranted judgments.

But J. Robert Hunter, president of the National Insurance Consumer Organization, told the committee the crisis is not caused by the courts and the lawsuits, but by the mismanagement and investment decisions of the insurance companies. Hunter said the medical malpractice insurance companies earned as much as 22 percent annually on net worth between 1976 and 1983—"almost double the average for all industries."

Myron J. Bromberg, a Morristown, New Jersey, lawyer who specializes in medical malpractice cases, said the shifting of the burden of proof from the plaintiffs to the defendant doctors has been the biggest cause of the medical malpractice insurance crisis.

Robert L. Van Fossan, Chairman of Mutual Benefit Life Insurance Company, told a New Jersey state senate committee that the courts have "converted what used to be a fault-based system" into a system that "now compensates for any and every injury no matter what the degree of fault of the entity called upon to make payment."

He called on the legislature to change the legal doctrine of joint and several liability to correct this and require payment only by each defendent of a share of the total judgment commensurate with its share of the blame. Van Fossan also accused the courts of awarding damages for matters not provided for in the insurance policies.

The New Jersey legislature is considering a bill to change joint and several liability. This doctrine can open the way to many abuses. Let us say that X is injured by Y in an auto accident. There is no question but that Y is to blame, but Y has very little liability insurance and hardly any assets. If X's lawyer can discover even a minor fault in Y's car that could have had a minute part in the accident, X then sues both Y and the manufacture of the car, the dealer who sold the car and the garage that serviced it. Under the joint and several liability doctrine any one of these defendants and its insurance company can be forced to pay the entire cost of the accident.

Meanwhile, in an interview in *The New York Times*, Michael T. Gallagher of Houston, a spokesman for the trial lawyers, charged that if there is an insurance crisis in the United States it is because the casualty and liability industry is preparing for a period of "huge profitability."

Gallagher said personal injury lawsuits have declined by 10 percent since 1981. He said there have been only 1,600 personal injury judgments exceeding $1 million in the past fourteen years and for a nation of 240 million people that is not excessive.

More dramatically, Gallagher said the liability companies are making huge profits and are succeeding in concealing the profits by their bookkeeping methods. He said the industry had a profit of $2 billion in 1985, paid $2.2 billion more in policy dividends and managed to add $12.5 billion to its consolidated surplus. This surplus is a reserve to pay future claims, but Gallagher said its most immediate use is for investments and that the industry had $19.5 billion in investment income in 1985 plus $5.4 billion in realized capital gains.

He said the liability insurance companies' bookkeeping and reporting methods enabled them to postpone reporting huge amounts of income and profit and to adjust their underwriting loss figures to whatever they wanted them to show by putting in huge figures for "incurred but not paid" and "incurred but not reported" claims.

He charged that the companies have not yet presented any real evidence that they actually have suffered big underwriting losses.

He said that in seeking caps on claims and changes in the tort laws, the companies have "pushed for a reduction in people's rights without offering anything in return in the way of reduced rates . . . their goal is to eliminate people's rights and increase premium rates with no tax levies on the insurance companies."

In citing the cases of twelve out-of-state liability companies that have gone broke in the past year and defaulted on $56 million in New Jersey claims, New Jersey State Insurance Commissioner Kenneth Merin told the Newark *Star-Ledger* that mismanagement was the cause. These companies specialized in liability coverage for the trucking, liquor, drug store and some other businesses.

Merin said they went broke because many of them sold their insurance too cheaply several years ago to raise quick extra cash to pour into high yield investments. They overestimated the yield they would get on the investments and underestimated the amount of claims that would be filed against them by their policyholders.

The defaulted claims, when approved, will have to be paid out of a special fund set up in 1974 by all the property/casualty insurance firms operating in the state.

Insurance operations of companies in the property liability business tend to be sloppy. An example of this sloppy management is the practice of paying adjusters fees amounting to percentages of the settlements they approve. What incentive have the adjusters to hold settlement costs down?

Another sloppy practice is paying out very small claims without investigating them because it's cheaper that way, but this only encourages floods of new frivolous and fraudulent small claims that ultimately add up to a lot of money.

Instead of buckling down to the hard task of reframing management policies to cope with the problems, the companies raise premium rates, often astronomically, or pull out of difficult areas. They are unwilling to dip in and tackle the problems on a case-by-case basis.

This cynical attitude results in part from poor training of personnel. The people in the business simply don't care enough about their customers or about their own function in society to even begin to hunt for fair solutions to the critical problems. Instead they turn to the state legislatures, demanding help in the form of legal caps on the amounts the courts can award in malpractice and other liability cases.

Congress is at this time in the middle of adopting a "risk retention" law, which would permit all professional and businessmen and public and private institutions to form groups to self-insure against liability risks and to buy and sell the protection on a group basis. A similar law was passed in 1981 applying to manufacturers only.

Theoretically, this could cut premium costs drastically, but critics of the plan say it can't work unless Congress also imposes a cap of, say, $250,000 on the amount the courts can award for pain and suffering. Congress shows no inclination to impose such a cap. Critics also say the risk retention groups would be underfinanced and in danger of going broke quickly.

The great majority of us are not directly concerned with the malpractice and product liability crisis. We are concerned indirectly because huge increases in the cost of insurance forces up prices of the services and products we must buy. So do some other unpleasant aspects of the property/casualty insurance business.

We are bombarded nowadays with advertisements in print and on the air by companies engaged in direct selling—by mail. The clerks who process these policies have no insurance experience of the kind that an insurance agent or broker has. Some of these direct writing insurance companies are owned and controlled by conglomerate corporations.

This direct selling is supposed to cut the cost to consumers by "eliminating the middle man"—the agent. In reality, the clumsy policies of some of the bigger direct writing companies have contributed greatly to the sad disarray of many segments of the insurance business. Their big outlays on advertising and their huge sales volume have not reduced costs to the consumers.

For the consumer, direct mail selling of insurance policies is a stultifying failure. The companies' advertising is not truthful and their bad management actually has caused runaway increases in costs. They give their own customers and other claimants a very hard time and force them to sue in the courts to collect what is justly due them, further inflating costs by large and unnecessary legal expense.

Their services usually are slow and their settlements stingy compared to those of the companies that market their policies and operate their business through agents.

The efforts of consumer and professional groups and state officials and legislators to resolve the liability insurance crisis have met with little success so far because of the obstinacy of the companies.

West Virginia and Florida state officials recently testified about this before a New Jersey state senate committee. The officials confirmed Houston lawyer Gallagher's statement that the companies flatly refuse to offer any rate reductions in return for the help they want from the legislatures—caps on awards for pain and suffering and malpractice, sharp changes in the doctrine of joint and several responsibility, and other tort reforms.

When the West Virginia legislature passed a law requiring the companies to report their losses as they actually were related to their claim experience in the state, the companies began pulling out of West Virginia, cancelling existing policies. The Supreme Court enjoined the companies from cancelling the policies, but the legislators gave in and repealed the law on claim reporting.

The Florida legislature passed the same type laws, plus a mandatory rollback in liability premium rates by 10 percent. The companies have threatened to pull out and have sued in the federal courts to have the new Florida laws set aside.

This refusal to negotiate fair solutions of the crisis is aggravated by the companies' obvious lack of desire to reach reasonable compromises.

This haughty nineteenth-century public-be-damned attitude augurs ill for any early improvement in the situation.

Radio and television and some print media carry many advertisements for "quick" life insurance coverage for all, including older persons, without any medical examination and with "no questions asked."

The announcers make it sound simple, easy and modestly priced, but what they don't tell you is that they are offering high-risk life insurance, which costs a lot. It is structured and priced for persons with serious health problems that make them ineligible for standard life insurance, and the premium rates are as much as four to five times those for standard life insurance.

But because the ads don't say they are selling high-risk insurance, about half of those who answer the ads and buy this insurance are healthy persons who easily could get life insurance in the standard market from an agent for a quarter or even a fifth of what these high-risk policies cost.

Even those who have serious health problems may have to pay considerably more for these policies than they could purchase high-risk insurance for through an agent, because these companies drastically inflate the usual high-risk mortality tables on which rates are based.

A lot of the hospitalization and medical insurance policies sold on the air to supplement Medicare or Blue Cross/Blue Shield also are bad buys compared with what one can get through an agent and extremely bad buys compared with supplemental insurance purchased from one's employer on the basis of union negotiations.

Another bad buy is the group affiliation sales for term life insurance. A special deal is offered to the graduates of a series of universities or some other large group. But the special deal usually turns out to cost up to 40 percent more than the same amount of term insurance you can buy on a one-on-one basis from a reputable company.

As you can see in this chapter on insurance, one must really be on his or her toes to avoid being taken.

CHAPTER 8

# A Better Legal System

W HENEVER the subject of lawyers and the courts
came up in my conversations around the country there were
lots of raised eyebrows and even scornful laughter.

It was plain that lawyers and the courts do not have a good
reputation with the American public. Many said we no longer
are a nation governed by law but by men—to be precise, by
venal, unscrupulous lawyers and by narrow, indifferent, timid
and sometimes corrupt judges.

Many people appear to think that, between them, the
judges and the lawyers often twist the laws out of all sem-
blance to their original meaning.

After hearing these comments, I was not much surprised to
read that retiring Chief Justice Warren Burger had told the
1986 convention of the American Bar Association in New York
that lawyers have a poor public image. The Bar Association
convention produced another interesting tidbit of news. The
convention adopted a report saying that judges are not forceful enough, that they do not exercise control of their courtrooms and too frequently are led by the nose and are dictated
to by the lawyers practicing before them. This report went on

to say that judges not only should rule their courtrooms, but that they "should take a more active role in the conduct of litigation; they should see that cases advance promptly and without abuse."

The lawyers were also criticized in the report for the "filing of frivolous motions and complaints, asserting unfounded defenses, pursuing abusive discovery [tactics] and making unwarranted appeals that glut our system of justice."

But the implication was plain, the judges are to blame for letting the lawyers get away with too many delays and shenanigans.

Well, supposing that's true, who is really at fault? It was interesting to note that the convention's report failed to consider that John Q. Public must share the blame for the failure of this system. After all, we have a right to a jury trial, and to have that jury consist of our peers. Yet how often have we received a jury notice and became upset about serving as a juror and grasped for an excuse or way out. Yes, each of us believes our time is too valuable to serve, and yet we are quick to blame the lawyer, the judge and the system when a big verdict is rendered against the company we work for, or the neighborhood doctor, dentist or hospital is found liable and millions of dollars in damages are awarded against them.

In order for the legal system to work we must serve as jurors and we must participate in it. We must petition the courts and the legislatures of this country to enact laws which are for all the people, not the select few. We can and should be watchdogs for our court system, serving as liaison officers and demanding that the judges we elect are competent and capable jurists, and voting out of office those jurists who are not worthy of wearing the robe.

How does one get to be a judge? In some states judges are appointed, thus permitting political patronage to rule, but in most jurisdictions the people have the power to elect them. However, either way there is a problem. Usually the county or state bar association endorses a candidate for office and finds they are qualified, and this is communicated to the public. However, local bar associations have been remiss in their obligation to the public; for as lawyers appearing before the judiciary they are unwilling to take an unpopular stand against a judge who is incompetent or unfit for office because of the fear of recrimination.

In the federal courts, a lawyer gets to be a judge as a matter of congressional patronage and he is appointed by the president to serve for life. To be removed a judge must be impeached and then tried in Congress. Like his state court counterpart, a judicial nominee needs the recommendation of the local bar association to get his appointment confirmed. But once seated on the bench, he no longer is vulnerable to pressures from lawyers appearing before him as state court judges are.

It has occurred to me that if the judges and lawyers were to put in effect the reforms proposed in the Chief Justice's report, lawyers would lose fees and the ability to earn a prosperous living. While it is true that certain of the lawyers today enjoy amazing wealth, the majority of lawyers earn salaries which are commensurate with management. The legal profession has far too many lawyers and competition is fierce in the lower levels of the profession.

It has been said that lawyers hold the balance of power in the country, and that they hold it in an unbreakable grasp is equally obvious. In numbers, they compose a large, if not majority of representation in Congress and the state legislatures and either hold or are advisers to the key posts of all bureaucratic departments and agencies.

Of course, I know that thousands of lawyers and judges, almost certainly a majority of them, are not involved in this power grab by the profession's militants.

Family lawyers write wills and deeds, search land titles, work out compromises or go to court if necessary to settle di-

vorce cases or disputes over property, handle suits arising
from damage claims and patiently get people out of troubles
they have gotten into by carelessness or misfortune.

Most local judges preside over these matters in the main
and would never dream of trying to usurp the prerogatives of
the legislatures by making laws from the bench.

Most corporate lawyers and lawyers who work for government agencies are only interested in getting their mountains
of paperwork done and in being fair to the public in disputes.

Nevertheless, lawyers do make the laws and the rules and
regulations in the first place and they are able to make sure
that they are tailored to serve the lawyers' interests primarily,
not those of the general population.

So the lawyers can make the law, unmake it and twist and
distort it. They rule the country, not the law itself. Yet, despite these problems, our system of justice works, and each of
us can influence if not control it.

There is a constant stream of complaints from businessmen,
writers, scholars and politicians that in the past thirty years
that the courts have usurped the legislative powers of both
the federal and state governments.

Crusaders for liberal causes and rapid change in our society
hail this "lawmaking by the courts" as "a great step forward in
social progress," and there can be no doubt that some decisions of the Supreme Court have caused great advances. The
court struck down racial segregation, for example.

But you cannot allow the courts to simply innovate on the
law in defiance of the prerogatives of the legislative bodies
and still have a nation ruled by law.

The public is inclined to give the judges both the credit and
blame for this new phenomenon of creating innovative laws in
the courtroom. But hold on a minute, isn't it obvious that a
judge cannot initiate innovative laws? He can only rule on ar-
guments presented to him, often passionately, by lawyers.

Just as a woman cannot have an illegitimate child unless

some man impregnates her, a judge cannot give birth to bas-
tard laws unless he is given the opportunity by lawyers who
impregnate his mind with the seeds of the new laws. We
stress the importance of having strong laws and good judges,
yet how many of us are willing to raise our taxes so that state
court judges are provided with law clerks and a support staff
which will enable them to rule on a case with knowledge of
the law, and allow them the time to prepare a well reasoned
opinion. Despite our complaints, despite our belief that the
system is unfair, when was the last time we spoke to or even
wrote to our representative? We elect them on fancy slogans,
but fail to hold them accountable for their actions.

Two fairly obvious generalizations can be drawn by observing the system in action. In the criminal courts the system
creates a climate of extreme leniency because that is what is
most profitable to lawyers. The lawyers could not hope for a
continuous harvest of big fees in a legal climate that produced
many convictions and severe sentences. Under the lenient
climate, most offenders are acquitted, have their sentences
cut drastically by plea bargaining or escape sentencing by pro-
crastination. That creates a flood of repeat fees for new of-
fences from the same offenders for the defense lawyers.

In the civil courts, the exact opposite is true. A climate of
severity and huge, often monstrous, judgments is created because that is what generates big attorney's fees.

All over the country, the police and federal agents are frus-
trated because they say the courts will not even hear the cases
against many, perhaps most, of those they arrest. The courts
give reasons of cost or time or arbitrary reasons such as that
one should not be accused of hit-run driving unless he flees
more than one mile from the scene of the accident before sur-
rendering. "Panic" is accepted as an excuse for shorter flights.

Persons with justifiable civil complaints run into an all-
pervasive atmosphere of judicial indifference and intolerable
delays, and even after a verdict is handed down, it appears

that very few judges have the time or interest in seeing that their orders are carried out.

The indifference of judges to the needs and sufferings of the persons involved in many civil cases is degrading to American life, yet we continue to permit this to occur. Here is a letter printed in a Red Bank, New Jersey, newspaper that tells the story most succinctly:

> To the Editor:
> I read with interest your topic entitled "Order of the Court." It was informative, sad, but true. I and my family have experienced just about every facet that was mentioned in the article.
> After six appearances in court over a four-year period with different judges presiding each time, I regard our present court system as quite ludicrous and filled with many loopholes. Decisions are made with little reference to what has occurred in the past. More communication is needed with the welfare and probation departments.
> Liens, judgments and bench warrants are placed by one judge, then weeks later removed by another judge. Very frustrating to say the least. A great deal of time, money, anxiety, not to mention all the paperwork involved, and for what?
> The goal and objectives of getting support into a household are rarely accomplished. What's in store for me and my six children? Just like you said, "Work full time so my children can receive life's necessities."
> What about the court system? I say, "Bag the whole idea."
> A court order is only as good as the person it is issued to.
> [The signature was withheld.]

The same sort of indifference to people's needs marks the long drawn-out proceeding of much bigger civil cases, although it's hard to imagine anything really much bigger than support for six children. That this lady had to appear before six different judges in four years shows poor judicial organization. As another letter to the Red Bank *Voice* on the same topic said, the way child support cases often are handled is "ludicrous and horrible." Judges sometimes act as if they were living in a little world of their own and were content to be highly paid paper shufflers.

One big reason for this is plain neglect by the public. Both the courts and the police are starved by the taxpayers and political executives. In no other country in the world have the police and the courts been treated so niggardly as in the United States. In the communist countries, the police and the courts stand at the very top of the social and economic scale. Americans never have faced up to the fact that if you want justice you have to pay for it. We need more courts and judges at both federal and state levels. Then perhaps judges could really try to speed things up and clear their calendars.

However, we need to do a lot more than spend money to again become a nation ruled by law. We should learn from the superior performance of our federal courts and do away with all popular election of judges. Appointed judges would be chosen by political patronage, but so, usually, are elected judges.

We also need to curb the excessive privileges lawyers have built up for themselves over the past three hundred years. Questions as to whether a defense lawyer should be permitted to knowingly plead a guilty defendant innocent should be resolved by having the lawyers take an oath they believe their clients to be totally innocent before pleading them not guilty. If the evidence then should indicate that the attorney knew the defendant was guilty, the matter could be referred by the judge to the grand jury on a charge of perjury. Why should the principle that the guilty as well as the innocent are entitled to representation by counsel be extended, as now is the case, to giving defense attorneys a carte blanch for deceiving the court and inducing witnesses to commit perjury or disappear so they cannot testify? Good question. Again, under our system of law, the prosecution must prove his case, but shouldn't he be paid a commensurate salary as the defendant's lawyer? People don't want to pay that salary. Some people believe that trial lawyers should be deprived of all voice in the selection of jurors, that only the judge should be allowed to examine the jurors and remove any of them from the box. But with our overworked jurists is this what we truly want; or do we want our procedures conducted by a craftsman?

Most of all, we need a constitutional amendment or a federal statute limiting the basis of appeals in criminal cases to matters bearing directly on the guilt or innocence of the accused. *All appeals on procedural errors should be forbidden.* It also might be well to require the appellate courts, if they accept a case for review, to resolve it outright instead of remanding it for a new trial in the lower court.

Our whole legal system is an adversary system, so it is only a modern extension of medieval trial by battle, when two armed knights representing the two sides fought a duel, often to the death, under the superstitious doctrine that God would award victory to the champion of the righteous cause. The modern adversary court trial also is a battle of naked power and deceit. The theory is that out of this modern trial the truth will emerge and justice will be dispensed. In the courts of this land it does happen much of the time, probably most of the time, but it is not what the lawyers intend. They are only interested in winning by any means, fair or foul, and care little about truth or justice.

The adversary system does not work as well in the civil courts as in the criminal courts because it becomes impossible to unravel the complexities of the issues sufficiently for either the jury or the judge to understand them completely. Nobody ever is satisfied with the verdict in a complicated civil case whether it is tried before a jury or simply decided by a judge.

We need a better system.

But it will be terribly difficult to find and establish a better system. The administered justice systems of the past, including those in effect in our own colonial era, were harsh and arbitrary. They were speedy, though, and the law generally was upheld and enforced in the criminal trials, although a lot of innocent persons were convicted and put to death. Civil trials too often were decided by bribery or naked "interest," that is, the litigant with the most relatives or friends in high places automatically was adjudged the victor, no matter what the law said.

As many people have told me in my travels, you can have the best case yet lose it if the opposing lawyer is more suave with more connections.

The communist countries still have administered systems of justice. There are no civil courts worth speaking of in these countries because there is no private property and nearly every kind of dispute that one might file a lawsuit over in America is decided automatically by the bureaucracy.

Communist criminal law is police state law. The police alone determine the guilt or innocence of a suspect by extremely harsh methods. A trial then is held merely to compel the defendant to recite his confession in public and to formally assess the punishment. Once in a while the judge and jury decide the police have made a mistake and that the defendant already has been punished enough, so he or she is acquitted.

But there is no pretense that the judiciary is independent of the police or of the state or communist party executives.

So, we are forced to conclude that, as a wit once said about democracy, our adversary legal system "is the worst of all possible systems—except all the others."

The reason it has lasted almost three hundred years is because no one has been able to think of anything better. But we have to find a better system or at least greatly improve it or the rule of law will perish in America, and so will truth and justice.

I do not pretend to know how to build a new legal system or to repair the existing system, but I do know that nothing can be done without your participation. We must deprive lawyers of the excuse that their actions are for the sole benefit or responsibility to their clients. We must provide support for our public defender system, our state attorney system and legal aid program. We must also require our schools and our universities to teach us basic law so that we are not in awe or in fear of the system. The law is for and by its citizens and we must help to make it work better. We are a force to reckon with.

CHAPTER 9

# The Armaments Juggernaut

FOR MORE THAN a dozen years now a bitter controversy has raged over the vast size of our defense program—and over the extravagance, arrogance and corruption of the Pentagon-industrial complex.

The struggle has continued even though defense spending has fallen from 9 percent of the gross national product in 1968 at the peak of the war in Vietnam to about 5 percent today. It has been sharpened in recent years because of the espousal by President Reagan and Defense Secretary Caspar Weinberger of the Star Wars program, which could cost hundreds of billions of dollars over a long period.

According to one's moral and political beliefs, the Star Wars idea either is a hope for a long era of peace in the world or it is the most monumental piece of folly and evil ambition ever conceived by the human mind. The fate of Star Wars ultimately will be influenced and could be decided in a summit meeting, and Soviet leader Mikail Gorbachev or the American electorate could step in and decide the issue in the 1988 presidential election.

Meanwhile, the nature of the struggle against the arma-

ments juggernaut is broadening and shifting. Added to the evidence of extravagance and corruption are charges of gross
and sometimes deliberate inefficiency in our armed forces and
the Department of Defense, charges that we do not have military or naval forces in readiness for emergency combat action
in spite of all the hundreds of billions of dollars given the military and the defense industries.

These charges that our armed forces are so badly trained
and badly commanded that they are a "paper tiger" were first
made by the enemy during the war in Vietnam. Now, they
are being echoed stridently by some of our own officers and
some civilian military scholars and experts.

During the Vietnam war, the charges, even when occasionally made by American officers and soldiers, did not attract
much attention. But in 1986, it became apparent that a scandal was building up far surpassing the public row kicked up by
Brig. General Billy Mithcell in 1925 when he charged that the
airplanes the Army was buying were no more than "flaming
coffins," totally useless for combat. Mitchell was crucified by
the brass; first he was demoted, and then kicked out of the
service when he refused to shut up. He tried for a political
career, but failed and died comparatively young. Ironically,
some of the same brasshats who crucified Mitchell made
speeches praising him and named an attack bomber for him
during World War II.

Today, we have a lot of Billy Mitchells, some in civilian
clothes, warning us that our expensive new weapons systems
are worthless, that many of our general officers are selfish, incompetent careerists, that Army enlisted men are too poorly
educated and badly trained to cope with modern weapons
and, worst of all, there is nothing in the whole philosophy and
structure of the armed forces to motivate young men to fight
for the country or to want to be good soldiers, sailors or air-
men.

Some of these modern-day Billy Mitchells are being

crucified as he was by the military brass and by the greedy, unscrupulous defense contractors. An editorial in *The New York Times* of August 11, 1986, tells the story of one of these, Air Force Colonel James Burton, whose determined criticism of the Army's Bradley Fighting Vehicle, which is meant to carry troops into battle, resulted in his forced early retirement.

There is no indication that Colonel Burton used any phrase resembling Billy Mitchell's "flaming coffins," but while serving as a test supervisor for the Defense Department he concluded the Bradley, as presently designed, was too dangerous to carry troops into battle because the crew was not segregated from the fuel supply and ammunition supply so a hit from a standard anti-tank weapon would ignite the fuel and ammunition and roast the crew to death. He said the problem could be solved by redesigning the vehicle and putting the fuel tanks and ammunition bins on the outside,where they would be separated completely from the crew.

But that would require halting production of the Bradley, and the Army didn't want that. "Congress might sour on the program altogether," the *Times* editorial remarked.

Congressmen Denny Smith of Oregon and Mel Levine of California took up Burton's charges and forced a test under simulated battlefield conditions of the Bradley. "The test confirmed the fears that the Bradley is a rolling powder keg," the editorial said.

Still the Army did not accept Colonel Burton's proposal. Instead it proposed "some quick fixes like an inside liner and explosive armor, then proceeded to test this version of the Bradley. The *Times* editorial goes on to say, "the tests were stopped, Colonel Burton claims, because at the last minute cans of water were substituted for the ammunition boxes," thus rigging the tests to make the vehicle look good.

Senator David Prior of Arkansas now has joined Congressmen Smith and Levine in a move to require new survivability tests for the Bradley using both Colonel Burton's proposal and the quick fix. Congress then can decide what to do. But Colonel Burton has been forced to retire from the service. Senator Prior said, "It's not Colonel Burton we should be trying to get rid of but those who have tried to rig tests."

The people I talked with on my travels were not aware of Colonel Burton's existence but they did know about the glaring failures of our military in recent years. They knew that combat performance in Vietnam did not measure up to the standards set in World War II although they were not sure about the reasons for that.

They felt much more certain about the failure of President Carter's hostage rescue effort in Iran—"too small a force," "not very good planning" and "the helicopter crews don't seem to have been well trained."

They were very certain about the shocking suicide bombing of the marine barracks at the embassy in Beirut that killed well over two hundred marines—"Just plain carelessness" and "The officers in charge were negligent and incompetent, no matter what the official report says."

They also were chagrined and humiliated at the way we had to use a "steam hammer to crack a walnut" in invading the tiny Caribbean island of Grenada in 1983—"and even then it took too much time and cost too many lives." There were also conflicting views about the political wisdom and morality of invading Grenada at all.

The most severe criticism of the efficiency of our armed forces and the defense establishment appears in a new book entitled *The Straw Giant* by Arthur T. Hadley. Although he served as a tank officer in World War II, Hadley is not a professional soldier. He is a military journalist and war correspondent. He cites six basic and fatal flaws in our overall defense setup:

1—Military and naval officers have become divorced from the general population. Consequently they tend to be looked on with contempt by the financial, general business, political and intellectual elites of society as unwanted and possibly vicious stepchildren.

2—Intraservice and interservice rivalry and infighting is so fierce and intense that many officers are totally preoccupied with it. This is destructive to morale and efficiency.

3—Organization is horrible. Nothing can be done without going through layer on layer of military and congressional bureaucracy. In consequence, worthwhile projects are whittled or watered down until they lose all their value.

4—It may be a source of chagrin to male ego to learn that the average female soldier is better educated and more efficient than the average male in uniform. But it's true. Therefore, we need a lot more women in uniform.

5—The all-volunteer army is not working out because too many of the volunteers come from the most disadvantaged levels of our society. Many of them cannot learn to read and understand a weaponry manual, much less how to fire the weapon so as to hit a target. Hadley says this means we must return to some kind of compulsory military service in order to get enough adequately qualified men and women in uniform. The Soviet Union relies on compulsory military service. So do Israel, West Germany and most of the uncommitted nations.

What makes this so necessary is that weaponry has changed more in the last fifty years than in many centuries. Hadley said today's soldiers and sailors must think and act in microseconds instead of hours and minutes.

The popular columnist James T. Kilpatrick says Hadley's descriptions of the bungled development and procurement of aircraft and weapons "makes painful reading."

Adam Yarmolinsky, chairman of the Committee for National Security, a civilian organization, adds a seventh and possibly more devastating basic criticism to Hadley's six. Yarmolinsky says the generals, Defense Secretary Weinberger and even President Reagan have their defense priorities upside down. "They are so fixated on major weapons, especially nuclear weapons, that they are willing to starve everything else."

He says readiness for combat in an emergency appears to be at the bottom of the Defense Department's priority list and that this is shown by the final defense budget for fiscal 1987—"the proposal cuts spare parts purchases for the Air Force by 39 percent, for the Army by 32 percent and for the Navy by 22 percent. Funds for ammunition, tactical missiles, and critical support equipment were slashed almost as deeply.

Yarmolinsky goes on to say that if the present top priority continues to be given to nuclear weapons while overall military spending remains level, the national security will become dependent on "weapons no one can use." He says that "even in an era of restrained defense spending we must maintain strong balanced forces," and this means having forces in readiness to fight—"Sacrificing the readiness of our conventional forces on the altar of nuclear modernization will undermine the flexibility and credibility of our military posture."

Another Pentagon weapon failure was described recently in *The New York Times* by Andrew Cockburn, a free-lance writer. It is the Stinger, a shoulder-held, heat-seeking anti-aircraft missile made by General Dynamics Corporation and sold to the Defense Department for $80,000 each. It is supposed to match the Soviet SAM-7, which the Arabs used against the Israelis in the 1972 Yom Kippur War.

But Cockburn says both the Russians and we have goofed on shoulder-held, anti-aircraft missiles. He says, actually, the Arabs only managed to down two Israeli planes with SAM-7s (they hit twenty-five) although they fired five thousand of the missiles at Israeli aircraft.

He says the Stinger has been an equally sad failure for the Afghan rebels to whom it was supplied. They have fired a great many Stingers at Soviet planes, as many as eighteen at a single aircraft, and as of mid-1986, not one Stinger had hit its target. A predecessor of the Stinger, the Redeye, supplied to the government of Chad, was a dismal failure when used against Colonel Khadafy's air force during the Libyan invasion of Chad.

The Army lately has introduced a program designed to correct one of its organizational deficiencies, but it is meeting with resistance. The new program is designed to promote cohesion or unit stability by cutting down on the prevailing huge transfer rate. The Army sometimes has personnel turnovers of 25 percent a quarter in combat companies. The Navy does much better in achieving unit stability because it's awfully difficult to train a ship's crew, so a skipper will fight like the devil to keep good men.

The German army always maintained high unit stability and the very efficient little Israeli army manages to keep men in the same unit for twenty years through their training, active service and reserve service periods.

The importance of unit stability becomes apparent if you ask yourself, What makes young men willing to fight and die in battle?There are several answers to the question but the most convincing one is that men will fight for other men they depend on and who depend on them, men they know well, their buddies. Why should an infantry platoon fight well for a lieutenant who only joined the company day before yesterday and may be transferred out again in a couple of weeks? Most of the soldiers won't even bother to learn the fellow's name, much less feel any loyalty to him. And if nearly all the men in one's squad are total strangers, there hardly can be much *esprit de corps* or willingness to stand and fight and die to protect the rest of the squad.

This lack of unit stability in our Army began in this century, in World War I to be exact, when so many whole new divisions and other combat units had to be formed overnight. In the nineteenth century, unit stability was strong. That it ought to be restored seems obvious, but a lot of officers and noncoms are very much opposed to unit stability for a very selfish reason. They like the fluid situation of frequent transfers because they think transfers mean career mobility and that career mobility leads to upward mobility, more rapid promotion. Never mind if the fluidity undermines combat effectiveness.

Every month or so we read in the newspapers of a new scandal involving vast overcharges and gross inefficiency on the part of defense contractors and Pentagon officers. The contractors involved in these scandals of waste, extravagance, fraud and careless design include some of the biggest corporations in the country. The overcharges we can easily lay to greed and fraud, but the reasons for the incompetence, bad design and bad manufacturing performance are not so easy to grasp.

There was a revealing report recently of an incident that sheds some baleful light on that. An ex-convict who was a high school dropout was disclosed to have got himself hired and to have worked as an engineer for two of the most prominent defense contractors, Lockheed and Northrop, through forged credentials. Were these forged documents checked on at all?

President Eisenhower, who certainly was a good professional soldier, warned us in his last days in the White House against the danger of creating a military-industrial complex that could turn into a juggernaut and destroy us. His warning was not heeded and his prophesy has come true, although we are not actually destroyed as yet. But the juggernaut is a terrible monster. Its wasteful arrogance knows no bounds of authority or common sense.

The spending of hundreds of million dollars on capital ships for the Navy that are sitting ducks for land-based or airborne missiles, as the British discovered in the brief Falklands war, is just one example of the juggernaut's arrogant folly.

However, nearly all Americans believe in a strong defense and there is a valid reason why all of our recent presidents (except Carter) accepted increases in defense costs. That reason is the paranoid conduct of the Soviet Union. Josef Stalin's aggressive expansionism from 1938 until his death in 1953 was continuous and brutal. He seized all of Eastern Europe and Manchuria at the end of World War II and tried to get control of China and Korea. His successors have gained effective control of Cuba and have fomented bloody civil wars in Asia, Africa and Latin America.

The origins of Russia's paranoia go all the way back to the Middle Ages when the Orthodox Church taught that anything that was not traditionally Russian was heretical and a mortal sin. The church insisted on total isolation for Russia.

This paranoid attitude was greatly reinforced by Napoleon Bonaparte's bloody and unprovoked invasion of Russia in 1812. The Russians won the war but their losses were frightful.

The Crimean War in the middle of the nineteenth century in which Britain, France, Turkey and Sardinia attacked Russia on a slender pretext, hardened the Russian fear and dislike of the west. So did the humiliating defeat in 1905 at the hands of the westernized Japanese. Hindsight tells us that the overreaction of the western allies, including President Wilson of the United States, to the Bolshevik revolution of 1917 was a great mistake. Sending western troops to Russia in 1918 ostensibly to protect foreigners seems today to have been stupid and malevolent, and the prolonged diplomatic and economic quarantine imposed on the new Soviet Union also seems today like tragic folly. It solidified the anti-western psychology in the Soviet Union.

Things were not helped when President Roosevelt and General Eisenhower rejected Winston Churchill's proposal for a second front in the east in World War II that would have

eased the pressure on the Soviet armies. Churchill's real
motive was to prevent Soviet armies from overrunning all
Eastern Europe, which they eventually did.

However, not all western observers believe Russian paranoia is only a result of fear and resentment of old wrongs.
Many think the Russians behave the way they do because of
their absolute commitment to Marxist dogma, the fervent belief that the whole world must be converted to Communism,
by force of arms if need be, and that any act of treachery or
aggression is justified if it will further the Communist goal.
President Reagan's public utterances sometimes indicate that
this is his view.

It seems certain that Defense Secretary Weinberger and
many in the Pentagon and the Army and Navy also subscribe
to this view of Soviet paranoia. So do some members of our
diplomatic corps and some of our business and intellectual
elites.

But if the President and the Pentagon chiefs believe this,
why do they assign such a low priority to having defense
forces in readiness to fight? Are they convinced that the only
thing we can do is build up our nuclear weapons and say to
the Soviets, look, if you destroy us we will destroy you in our
death throes?

If that is our position, it is a pessimistic and defeatist position and we have not historically been a pessimistic or defeatist nation.

During my travels I was primarily feeling the nation's economic pulse, but people insisted on talking about many other
things and nothing appeared to concern them more than the
possibility of nuclear warfare.

Except for a few paranoiacs of our own, the people don't
want us ever to drop another atomic bomb on any people anywhere. That's positive.

But when it comes to how to avert a nuclear war, they are
divided on the question of whether we should continue our

nuclear buildup and back the President's Star Wars plan or should scale down the nuclear program and put our faith in negotiating with the Russians and maintaining strong conventional forces in readiness for emergencies.

I found that opposition to the nuclear weapons buildup clearly is growing in the population now, and so is skepticism about the feasibility and wisdom of Star Wars.

After World War II, it seemed to the Russians that the United States had erected a ring of offensive military naval bases around the world aimed at them. Actually the bases were built originally for the containment and destruction of German and Japanese forces and were not aimed at the Soviet Union, and their continuance in peacetime was in theory to prevent a resurgence of military aggression from any quarter, but that's not how it seemed to the Russians. We should remember that Russia's war experiences were far worse than ours. Her casualties and damage at Hitler's hands were frightful enough to give every living Russian a new reason to fear the west.

But Russian children have it drummed into them from early childhood that capitalism (free enterprise) inevitably leads to war and that the ruling classes in all capitalist countries are willing and even eager to take their populaces into war against the communist world.

That is the crux of the matter. If we want to get rid of the armaments monkey on our backs we must find a way to convince the Russians that we never will attack them, and convince them that the Marxist idea of a communist world is unworkable and unachievable. Actually Karl Marx would not have approved of the Stalinist idea of a world ruled by Moscow. It is doubtful if Nicolai Lenin would have approved of it either.

Some Soviet actions such as the prolonged war in Afghanistan seem almost totally incomprehensible to Americans and most other western peoples. If that costly struggle has demonstrated anything it is that Afghanistan's rugged mountains and its equally rugged people never could serve as a springboard for an invasion of Russia.

For another excellent reason, we should desire peace and prosperity for the Russians as well as for ourselves. Generally speaking, nations do not launch wars when they are prosperous and feel sure of continued stability. There have been many exceptions to this rule because there have been a great many megalomaniac or paranoid rulers in the world, but the peoples themselves do not become warlike until they begin to suffer or feel immediately threatened. It is when times are bad and danger seems close and real that it is easy for rulers to get the common people to follow the flag and march into battle.

There are some other unpleasant aspects of our defense juggernaut.

Defense expenditures are the most inflationary outlays man can be guilty of. So long as we have a big armaments program we never can be sure that runaway inflation won't again rear its ugly head.

The output of arms is profitable but it is not productive for society. It does nothing in itself to maintain or improve the quality of life. On the contrary it makes possible massive terrorism and fratricidal religious and civil wars, and keeps in power dictators and tyrants all around the globe. The United States not only manufactures vast quantities of weapons, we sell them to many other nations and sometimes lend them the money to buy the weapons. We do this for the ostensible purpose of maintaining stability and containing communism. Many other countries, Israel, France and Sweden, for example, make and sell arms and so do the countries of the Soviet bloc. Russia lends her client states money to buy Soviet arms.

Large corporations get most defense contracts, so a huge defense program favors big business and decreases competition in the economy.

A big defense industry does create new inventions that later become useful, even revolutionary, in the civilian economy. But on the whole, big armaments production is the most wasteful activity ever conceived by man and morally the most destructive and stultifying.

We must find ways to whittle it down drastically.

# CHAPTER 10

# Crime, Narcotics and Pornography

**W**E READ and hear a little less about crime now than a few years back, but more about drug addiction and drug trafficking.

People I met during my recent travels confirmed this impression and they were quick to give President Reagan much of the credit for the drop in crime.

"He hasn't accomplished any miracles but he has put us back on the right track," was a typical comment. "He appoints judges and officials who aren't soft on crime"—"He has the Justice Department running down real criminals instead of wasting its time on foolish anti-trust suits and persecuting business by tough enforcement of a lot of ill-considered regulations," were others.

Of course Mr. Reagan hasn't accomplished any miracles; after all, ordinary crime prevention is the province of the state governments, but his administration has set a good example for the states simply by being stern.

Statistically, the drop in crime rates is not very impressive and the streets, parks and buildings in New York and a few

other cities still are not safe for respectable citizens to wander
around in alone at night.

The ultimate cause of crime is not known. If we could discover this ultimate cause, we could do a much better job of
controlling crime. The deprivation theory, that crime is
caused by poverty and neglect, still is the most popular idea
and certainly a high proportion of those who commit crimes
come from impoverished backgrounds. But as the ultimate
cause, the deprivation theory does not stand the tests of hard
logic and historical experience. For example, it can't explain
most white collar crime that seems to be caused by pure
greed.

The theory that all criminals are psychotic doesn't get us
very far because psychiatry is not an exact science. The idea I
expressed in Chapter 2 that all criminals are infantile is true,
but many infantile persons do not become criminals and we
don't know what makes so many persons remain infantile
most of their lives.

We do know that an important cause of crime is that it is
easy to get away with in our country. The Citizens Crime
Commission of New York estimated in 1982 that the chances
of being caught and convicted for any given offense were only
one in 5,600. Things haven't changed a lot in five years.

But if we don't know the ultimate cause of crime, we do
know the immediate causes or the conditions with which
crime is most frequently associated. Poverty probably is the
most important but it is closely rivaled by alcohol abuse in all
levels of society, racial discrimination, ignorance, narcotics,
violence in television programs and movies, and the excessive
permissiveness of modern society in sexual and other aspects
of life—the lack of discipline in the home and at school.

In the past quarter century, a quantum increase in rape and
other sexual sadism, and the sexual abuse and exploitation of
children point a finger squarely at pornography and violence
and absence of ethical values on TV and movie screens.

The Reagan administration's stern and determined struggle against crime has been most apparent in two areas—white collar or business crime and trafficking in narcotics. Both of these usually fall under Federal jurisdiction, white collar crime because it frequently involves violation of the postal and federal securities control laws.

White collar crime may not have actually decreased during the Reagan years—new scams pop up every month—but the detection and prosecution of these thieves and swindlers has reached new highs.

Although all the states have anti-narcotic laws, the federal government agencies have the primary responsibility for suppressing the drug evil. Under the Reagan administration, seizures of large quantities of heroin, cocaine and marijuana and arrests and prosecutions of dealers have increased dramatically.

The administration lately has adopted a new tactic against users of crack, the new smokable form of cocaine. Federal law permits the confiscation of automobiles in which narcotics are seized. In the past, this law has been invoked only against dealers, but lately it has been used against users of crack and it could be applied against other customers of the drug peddlers—cocaine users, for example. This new tactic is confiscation of the users' automobiles when only a small amount of the drug is found in their cars. Since automobiles are involved in a majority of user purchases of cocaine, this tactic might prove quite effective. The user whose automobile is confiscated will suffer a severe immediate financial loss. The only way he can retrieve the car is to buy it back at a government auction for cash and the prices at such auctions are not cheap. If, as usually is the case, a bank or finance company has a lien on the car, it still must be paid off. Since the finance company can no longer repossess the car, it will slap new liens on any other property the chap may have and garnishee his wages.

If he doesn't go to jail and needs a car to keep his job, the crack user must find and buy a cheap jalopy to get to and from work and keep his job.

The chances of getting caught when using an automobile in making a drug buy are somewhat higher than when buying from a street pusher. If the federal authorities extend this confiscation tactic to users of drugs other than crack, it could cause a lot of cocaine users to decide that the financial risk is too great and kick the habit.

The administration also has obtained the reluctant cooperation of some Latin American governments in choking off the production of marijuana and cocaine at the source—the jungle plantations and jungle processing laboratories. The reluctance of the Latin American governments grows out of the fact that cocaine, marijuana and heroin are their principal sources of hard money income and that some thousands of farmers in their remoter rural areas have no other way of making a living.

So even if a considerable number of these jungle plantations and laboratories are destroyed, they are sure to be back in production in a few weeks or months.

Even if the use of cocaine, heroin and marijuana were to be greatly reduced, we still would have to contend with a flood of synthetic drugs, amphetamines and others, including the hallucinogenic drugs such as LSD. These are sold mainly on college and high school campuses by student pushers who are supplied by criminal dealers.

Some of these drugs are imported but many are made in clandestine laboratories under no supervision here at home. Some are pain relievers, others are pep pills or growth pills. Practically all of them are chemical time bombs in the human body and may cause serious disorders in future years. Athletes are particularly prone to use them.

Although his administration is prepared to spend millions of dollars to try to suppress the production and smuggling into the United States of narcotics, President Reagan has courageously warned the nation that crippling the drug traffic won't stamp out the narcotics evil or even greatly ameliorate the problem. He said the only way the drug epidemic can be conquered is by "taking the customers away from the dealers and producers," not just by attempting to suppress the supplies.

In a broadcast news conference in August, 1986, he said this has been accomplished before and can be again. He said the United States had a serious drug epidemic at the start of this century, then, in rather a short time, Americans quit their drug habits and stopped buying narcotics. It simply became socially unacceptable to fool with drugs. He said we can do that now and he called for a national crusade to stop the use of narcotics.

However, there are many differences between today's drug epidemic and the one at the beginning of the century.

The drugs used then are not nearly so addictive as those being used today. They were morphine, the common hospital pain killer, and cocaine. Morphine is not nearly so addictive as its derivative, heroin, the main hard drug used today. If it were, the hospitals simply couldn't use it. Nor is morphine anywhere near so dangerous to the human system as heroin, the monkey on the backs of the junkies today.

Cocaine is not highly addictive in the normal forms in which it is "snorted" or injected by a needle. Most cocaine users are thrill seekers rather than addicts. A few do become addicts, but we know now that cocaine is far more dangerous to the human heart, brain and lungs than has been supposed in the past.

Much of the new information about the deadly perils of using cocaine for any length of time has not yet found its way into the standard medical literature or into textbooks, according to the chief and assistant chief of medicine at the Bronx Veterans Administration Medical Center in New York. The two doctors explained the newly discovered perils of cocaine in a letter to *The New York Times.*

Crack, the new smokable form of cocaine, is extremely addictive and very dangerous and rapid in its action within the human system.

Marijuana, the most widely used drug today, was little known and seldom used in the United States in 1900.

Another difference between then and now is that there was no big money to be made out of smuggling or peddling drugs in 1900. Drugs were not illegal. Almost everywhere, one could walk into a drugstore and buy morphine or cocaine over the counter without a prescription.

But probably the biggest reason that the dope epidemic at the turn of the century was conquered so quickly is that Americans of that era were still rather puritanical and the authority of the clergy, the school teachers, the police and, above all, parents was enormously greater than it is now. From the pulpit, the teacher's desk, from the cop on the beat and at home everybody had it drummed into their ears constantly that playing with narcotics was not only terribly foolish, but it was also a mortal sin that would be punished by hell fire for a long, long time.

The people listened and harkened to these voices of religious, intellectual, civil and family authority. They turned away from narcotics. In those times even hardened criminals often had quite literal notions about hell fire. And we did not have another serious drug problem for the next sixty years.

It will be much harder to get the people to turn their backs on narcotics now.

But Mr. Reagan is not fazed by the difficulties. In calling for a national crusade against drug use, he seeks to involve both voluntary and mandatory action, including urinalysis testing for drugs in private industry as well as in government service. He also demanded a crackdown on drug use in the schools all the way from grammar school through the universities. In a nationwide broadcast in mid-August, 1986, the President said, "I believe we have come to a time when the American people are willing to make it clear that illegal drug use and alcohol abuse no longer will be tolerated."

"It is time to go beyond government," he continued. "All the confiscation and law enforcement in the world will not cure this plague as long as it is kept alive by public acquiescence."

A White House spokesman said Mr. Reagan favors extending the mandatory drug testing procedures already in force in the armed forces and some other government services to all private corporations. That will arouse considerable resistance.

The goal of the President's crusade is to get three to five million cocaine users, up to ten million heroin addicts and up to 20 million who smoke marijuana regularly or now and then off the drugs. Marijuana is not highly addictive but the damage it can do and frequently does to the human body is seriously underestimated by pot smokers, according to standard medical opinion. The President said that providing adequate treatment for those who are addicted to any drug will be an important part of his program. With most of the cocaine and marijuana users it's just a habit, not an addiction, and can be broken simply by the desire to do so. It is easier than breaking the cigarette smoking habit, for tobacco is much more addictive than either cocaine or marijuana.

Mr. Reagan listed five other goals for his crusade:

—A drug free workplace for every American.
—Drug free schools.
—International cooperation to suppress drug trafficking.
—Strengthened law enforcement.

—Expanded public awareness to make drug use socially unacceptable anywhere.

The President defended his insistence on wide mandatory testing by noting that its adoption by the armed forces already has reduced drug usage in the forces by 67 percent.

He said that one reason he feels confident of the ultimate success of the crusade is that there already are more than ten thousand "Just Say No" clubs among young people throughout the country. The "Just Say No" phrase was posed dramatically some years ago by Mrs. Reagan in California. Nancy became seriously concerned about drug addiction in the country long before Ronald.

"If this battle is to be won—and it must be," Mr. Reagan said, "each and every one of us has to take a stand and get involved. Leadership and commitment must be evident not only in the White House and the state houses, but also in the pulpit, at the work place, in the union hall and in the schools and in the media."

We have had a big increase in rape, sexual abuse and exploitation of children, and in wife beating and other domestic violence in recent years. Since this criminal surge has coincided with the growing up of an $8 billion a year industry producing and distributing pornographic literature, photographs and films, there is a natural tendency to blame the increase in the crimes on the spread of the pornography.

After a year's study, a panel appointed by President Reagan's attorney-general, Edward Meese, has come up with a report saying that, indeed, pornography is largely to blame. This report flatly contradicts a report made in 1970 by a commission named by President Nixon. The 1970 report said there was no evidence that pornography causes rape or other criminal behavior.

Many psychiatrists, psychologists, criminologists and law enforcement officials have expressed the view that rapists, at least violent rapists, are not motivated by sexual desire, they are motivated by a psychotic hatred for women, a craving for power and indulgence in cruelty, so pornography aimed at stimulating sexual lust would have little influence on them.

However, a significant portion of the pornographic litera- ture, pictures and films being sold today appeals to sadism and masochism and not to sexual desire. They include pic- tures of women in chains, trussed up in unnatural postures, women being whipped brutally by men and some of men be- ing whipped by women. This stuff could be a stimulant for the susceptible to carry out similar violence in real life.

But there is another kind of rape that is usually the result of unbridled sexual desire. It is non-violent rape, sometimes called "date rape." The violent rapist brutally beats or even kills his victim and usually threatens her with a knife or a gun and he is very rarely known to the victim. The "date" rapist, on the other hand, is known to his victim. He does not beat her or threaten her. He simply overpowers her and has his way with her.

Pornography plainly can and almost certainly does stimu- late sexual desire in males sufficiently to cause the big in- crease in date rape.

That pornography is responsible for the growth of the sex- ual exploitation of children cannot be doubted because that's where the money is. Children of both sexes are recruited, ei- ther seduced by money or intimidated by adults—very often by their own parents—to pose naked and to engage in explicit sexual acts before the still or motion picture camera, mostly with each other, occasionally with adults. This stuff is de- signed to stimulate the sexual fantasies and the libidos of those who view it. The photos and films also can stir up latent tendencies towards sadistic cruelty to children.

However, the report of the Meese panel is vulnerable to other criticism. It calls for specific actions against pornographers, some of which would clearly violate civil rights and, according to Barry Lynn, legislative counsel of the American Civil Liberties Union, "would amount to censorship and violate the First Amendment guaranty of free speech."

The report lists thousands of books, magazines and films that the panel members think should be banned.

The report bases its conclusions on the panel members' own observations and the national experience rather than on the views of scientific experts. It appears to suggest that the American experience with pornography and sexual permissiveness is paralleling that of Sweden. During the 1950s popular sentiment in Sweden demanded complete sexual freedom. Consequently, beginning in 1960, Sweden repealed all laws against pornography, public nudity and other sexual restraints. People began indulging in sex in parks and on the beaches. The sale of pornographic literature was right out in the open and it boomed. Swedish television and movies were replete with explicit sexual acts. An explicitly physical sex education program was introduced in all the schools.

Soon there was a huge increase in teen-age pregnancies and illegitimate births. These were accompanied by rises in alcoholism, drug addiction and suicide among the young.

The Swedes became alarmed, a Royal Commission was appointed to study the situation and the commission eventually came up with a report that rather quickly led to restoration of many of the old laws and customs. Some prominent Swedes who had been quite active in bringing about the sexual liberalization in the first place were among those demanding an about face and a return to the old morality as quickly as possible.

The increase in wife beating and other domestic violence can be blamed on many causes, firstly on the frustrations of the male unemployed. For example, when the jobless rate in

Youngstown, Ohio, rose to 21 percent in 1982, domestic violence offenses reported to the authorities soared by 400 percent over those in 1979.

Pornography may well have some part in this increase in domestic violence because its general impact is to degrade women and marriage.

But there is something else that is creating the kind of climate that fosters wife beating, cruelty to children and violent crime in general. It is the monstrously excessive display of violence on the television and motion picture theater screens. Popular fiction in paperback books is equally guilty of glorifying violence and cruelty.

Except for a few comedy shows and sporting events, there is almost nothing on commercial television except violence. The regular networks, the pay-TV cable systems and the independent stations all try to outdo each other in displaying blood and guts to their viewers. They and the film producers search frantically for ever newer ways to provide novelties in murder and mayhem. This is a stultifying competition.

The staggering thing about the violence is that so much of it is utterly mindless, it is just there to make up for the feebleness of the infantile story lines of the programs and give perverted thrills to the viewers.

The only "lift" the programs seek to give the viewers is the same as that of the movies, to display a falsely high material standard of living in the United States. Character is equated with wealth and happiness, with expensive clothes, automobiles and other material possessions.

Not even lip service is paid to the true dramatic and ethical values of the traditional theater.

But the programs provide vicarious thrills of the wrong kind to much vaster audiences than any entertainment could in the past. By glorifying violence so much and making it so much more important than dramatic acting and writing in the minds of the public, the programs have a degrading influence on society.

It is moral and intellectual defeatism, the depiction of an America that has no concern with moral standards, nobility of character or artistic beauty.

This is bound to be a big factor in the rise of crime.

What about the money cost of crime and narcotics? The true money loss to the nation of drug addiction cannot be calculated but some of the cost to the people of drug trafficking is included in the annual bill for crime, which was estimated in 1982 at $150 billion. It hasn't changed much since then. But another enormous cost of crime and drug addiction is not included in the $150 billion a year figure. It is the loss of so many small businesses in our cities that simply cannot continue to exist because of repeated holdups and burglaries.

Insurance becomes unaffordable to these businesses, and in the retail and professional fields they dare not stay open enough hours each day to do a volume sufficient to stay in business because of the crime rate. Customers won't come to their stores after dark anyway because the streets aren't safe from muggers. Federal and local officials say crime has destroyed more small businesses than inflation or recessions and that several million jobs have been lost by the small business closings.

Racketeering crime against larger businesses and municipalities also has cost a lot of jobs as well as huge amounts of money.

This kind of crime forces costs of products and services up so much that many larger firms simply trim their operations, laying off workers by the thousands.

Racketeering crimes by contractors, union officials, public officials and building materials suppliers is perhaps the biggest factor in the severe crisis in housing in New York and some other cities. By creating a devastating artificial shortage of housing, these crises force rents and purchase prices of co-operative and condominium apartments up astronomically.

It is also impossible to measure the added cost for goods and services caused by drug addiction on the job, slowing productivity, when employees work on only four cylinders.

Many persons laughed at Barry Goldwater when he campaigned for president on the issue that crime was the American people's biggest problem. Today all of us have to admit he was right.

# CHAPTER 11

# *Where We Stand*

**W**E AMERICANS can rejoice because we are one of
the few nations not rocked frequently by violent political
demonstrations in which many people are killed or wounded.

There are no threats of revolt or takeover plots worth
noticing in the United States. But if our budget and trade
deficits continue to grow as alarmingly as they have in recent
years, not only will our political prestige and power in the
world decline seriously but poverty will widen sufficiently at
home to cause a dangerous discontent that could lead to civil
turmoil.

However, I found in my lecturing tours that the American
public is most concerned about two things—the nuclear peril
and whether or not they will have security in their old age. By
nuclear peril I mean both the danger of nuclear war and the
risk of a disastrous nuclear power accident such as occurred at
Chernobyl in the Soviet Union. Such an accident would not
have to take place in our own country in order to do us great
damage, but the big fear I encountered was of a nuclear accident on our own soil caused by carelessness or neglect.

People also are very concerned about the risks from radiation from nuclear wastes that are inadequately disposed of.
They are as much concerned about the dangers of pollution
from ordinary chemical wastes, both the wastes being dis-

posed of now by mines and factories and those that have been
buried in our soil in the past century.

This deep public concern about the nuclear peril does not
bode well for the long-range political chances of President
Reagan's Star Wars program. I think a great many Americans
were impressed by Soviet leader Gorbachev's speech on August 18, 1986, in which he extended the Soviet Union's unilat-
eral ban on nuclear weapons testing.

But it was not the extension of the testing ban that impressed Americans. They accepted, in the main, our own government's judgment that Gorbachev "wasn't giving away
much." What was most impressive was Gorbachev's depiction
of the dire consequences of continuation of the arms race. His
most important statement was: "Today it is simply suicidal to
build international relations on the illusion of attaining superiority in terrible means of destruction. Experts have estimated
that the explosion of the smallest nuclear warhead is equal in
radioactivity to three Chernobyls. And if someone dares to
make a first nuclear strike, he will doom himself to agonizing
death—not from a retaliatory strike but from the consequences of the explosion of his own warheads."

Neither does the public's concern over the nuclear peril au-
gur well for the future of the nuclear energy industry. Nuclear
power has not lived up to its early promise. The capital cost of
the atomic fission plants has escalated too much and their reli-
ability record has been sufficiently unsatisfactory so that the
cost advantage of nuclear-generated electricity over hydroe-
lectric and fossil fuel powered generating plants has shrunk
substantially.

As this is being written, all five of the Tennessee Valley Authority's nuclear reactors have been shut down because of
safety deficiencies. This is expected to cost the TVA $200 mil-
lion for the purchase of replacement power from other utilities in 1986. There are a number of other shutdown or
unfinished atomic power plants around the country and some

giant nuclear power projects have been abandoned with huge losses to taxpayers and to stockholders and customers of the utilities involved.

During the summer of 1986 the Fusion Laboratory at Princeton, New Jersey, announced a great breakthrough that could bring fusion, the opposite of the present nuclear fission system, much nearer. Theoretically fusion could create man-made suns and achieve the ultimate goal of cheap, unlimited quantities of electricity. Not all nuclear scientists think this goal is achievable, however. The Princeton laboratory's announcement made the front pages and the major news telecasts and radio news programs but the reaction was almost nil. The public was neither stirred nor enthused.

On the other hand, stories in the newspapers or on the air about the perils of radiation and pollution from either atomic plants or ordinary chemical plants and mines and their waste disposal, past and present, got a huge and passionate response from the people, including many politicians. There were shrill demands for instant government action to cure the menaces and to punish guilty utilities and other corporations. The movement for a nuclear freeze obviously is gathering strength.

The public's growing fear of nuclear war is putting the Reagan Administration in a bind in its relations with the Soviet Union. The President was right in saying when he announced he was vetoing the 1986 armaments bill as passed by Congress, that Congress was giving away the bargaining chips he had hoped to use in dealing with the Russians at Geneva, but he probably was wrong in saying that this astounded the Russian leaders. They probably expected it. The Soviet government is a lot better at evaluating public opinion in the west and its probable impact on government decisions and actions than we are in evaluating their public opinion and its impact, if any.

In the first place, there are no organs or voices of public

opinion in the communist world and public opinion is not allowed to have any influence on the Communist Party or the Soviet Government. So, there is little for western governments and private observers to evaluate. Russia remains the same tyrannical enigma to western eyes that she always has been.

The Kremlin probably has noticed something that our government and the American people are reluctant to face up to—our network of allies in the world is crumbling, and a growing number of younger Americans are glad of it. The voices of these people are being echoed in Congress by proposals to bring home all or nearly all of the 330,000 troops we now have in Europe and reduce our total armed forces accordingly.

Our network of allies is crumbling because, with the exception of Israel, all the nations that have been so dependent on us for the last forty years are getting sick of us. They want to regain their total independence and go their own ways as they did before World War II. Like young birds eager to leave the nest, they do not aspire to return. They want to throw off American control and American influence permanently.

Although they are not allowed to talk about it, there is little doubt that the peoples in the eastern European satellite countries are just as eager to be free of Russian rule and to go their own way.

It is not the presence of American troops on their soil or strong anti-American feelings that is causing our west European allies to drift away. Anti-American sentiment is growing but it is not a vital force. The west Europeans want cultural and economic freedom from American influences as well as freedom from military dependence on us. A new wave of enthusiasm for pan-Europeanism also is sweeping the continent from Portugal to Greece and from Italy to Norway.

Most of all, Europeans, particularly the British, resent the way American corporations are buying up their industries.

They fume at the way they are being stripped of independent manufacturing capability, and they resent the Americanization of their societies and their cultures. For example, many French people bitterly resent the introduction of American-style restaurants. They say fast foods and standing up to eat are barbarous practices not to be tolerated in a civilized country.

The west European peoples and their governments do not share, or at least they do not share strongly, our officially held belief that the Soviet government intends to conquer the world for communism by force of arms.

Observing all this, Soviet officials undoubtedly feel these tendencies in the West will strengthen their hand in a summit meeting between Gorbachev and Reagan. That helps to explain why Gorbachev usually sounds so optimistic about making progress towards peace without offering anything in the way of concessions to the West.

I found people upset over our huge budget and foreign trade deficits because they fear the impact of the deficits ultimately will wipe out much of the purchasing power of their savings, their Social Security benefits and their pensions.

All the chatter of politicians, government officials, editorial writers, commentators and the economists on the nature and causes of the budget deficit seems horribly confusing but a few truths do stand out. The deficit problem began with President Lyndon Johnson's insistence on fighting a major war in Vietnam without putting the country on a wartime economic footing. The problem has worsened almost continuously ever since and is being aggravated by President Reagan's determination to cut taxes while increasing already high defense outlays enormously.

Right now the problem is being compounded by a sharp recession that has turned all the government's revenue assumptions topsy-turvy; also, assumptions about expenses have gone awry.

The Gramm-Rudman Budget Balancing Act is a slight but firm step in the right direction but basically such a mandatory automatic system is the least desirable way of cutting federal spending. Gramm-Rudman really is a mechanism to let senators and congressmen get the credit for voting to reduce spending without having to vote directly on anything that would cut government funds for anybody in their own bailiwicks.

Of course, the ideal solution would be for the members of Congress to vote on every individual proposed spending slash and vote on the basis of the national interest rather than the parochial desires of their constituents. But even thinking along those lines is pure wishful dreaming.

Ironically, President Reagan, whose policies have so aggravated the deficit problem, has proposed the only realistic solution—the item veto over budget and major appropriation bills. Congress has stubbornly refused to grant this, considering it a too palpable delegation to the executive of the powers given Congress in the Constitution.

But a recent editorial in the *Wall Street Journal* said the item veto is the only possible workable solution to the budget deficits: "Whether it happens now or after the elections the item veto will arrive. There is a growing will to tackle the budget problems and, at the end of the day, the item veto will be the only proposition on the table."

The most forceful statement in the editorial said, "The emerging consensus is that Congress is no longer capable of exercising the power of the purse over individual federal programs it enacted into law, nor does it want to exercise that power."

The *Journal* went on to say that Congress hoisted itself by its own petard because "its members assured themselves of incumbency with endless programs that created a universe of captive constituencies among the poor, the middle class, and U.S. business. . . . As a result, log rolling and the pork barrel, formerly a minor but survivable distortion of the political system, became the dominant feature of congressional politics."

Finally, the editorial concluded that authority for managing the federal budget will have to be vested in the executive: "The presidency remains the only federal institution with a broad enough constituency to make choices, and discipline the log rolling."

I didn't find people terribly knowledgeable about how the item veto might work and they were very divided about it. Many supported the idea but others, whose livelihoods depended on federal funding of local programs or enterprises, were fearful of it. Would it mean that their own senators and congressmen no longer could protect their jobs, their water supplies or other federal benefits from a White House veto?

Those I talked with were even more shocked and worried over the ever mounting foreign trade deficit, which could reach $175 billion for 1986. They just could not understand how American manufacturing and agriculture, so dominant in world markets only a few years ago, could fail so miserably and become so totally uncompetitive.

The failing dollar has failed to encourage the sale of made-in-America products in Europe and Japan as had been expected. The rise in the value of foreign currencies has not stopped Americans from buying a huge flood of foreign goods, including big ticket items like automobiles and aircraft, and cameras and sound systems.

Prices of American farm produce, while relatively low, still are too high to compete with those of other nations in a period when there is a global surplus of all agricultural products.

The assumptions about improving matters by lowering the value of the dollar were unrealistic as regards time. History shows that it takes quite a long time for a fall in the value of a nation's currency to correct a serious unfavorable trade imbalance.

I learned there is a growing populist movement in the country that favors protectionism—high tariffs on all imported products. President Reagan is vigorously resisting protectionism. He was a teen-ager and a struggling young adult during the Great Depression of the 1930s and he knows that most economists and historians believe that the undue faith in protectionism by the Harding, Coolidge and Hoover administrations played a major part in bringing that depression on.

So he recently vetoed a bill that would have reduced textile and apparel imports from a dozen countries by 40 percent. He pointed out that production in the American textile industry reached a record high in February, 1986.

The protectionist movement gained a bit of a lift from a new book by Robert Z. Lawrence and Albert E. Litan, economists of the Brookings Institution. They said our system of import quotas had failed to help American industry and save jobs and should be succeeded by across-the-board tariffs to help those industries that can show they have been hurt by foreign competition over a period of five years. The two authors said the voluntary quotas on importation of Japanese automobiles had enabled the Japanese to raise the prices of their cars on the American market and realize $2 billion to $4 billion in extra profit thereby.

There is no quick or easy way to wipe out the foreign trade deficit, but I discovered that many persons haven't yet accepted that. Nor do they accept the now proven idea that the American steel industry virtually committed suicide by depending on government protection instead of modernization. Other steel producing countries modernized their mills and grabbed the market.

There are a few encouraging signs. Imports of Japanese automobiles began falling in 1986 from the 1985 level. The surge of the yen against the dollar caused the Japanese to raise the prices of their cars about 15 percent. The Japanese automakers and their American dealers soon discovered that most Americans simply would not pay the additional 15 percent. So, for the first time since their massive invasion of the U.S. market began two decades ago, dealers in Japanese cars had to be flexible in their pricing, they couldn't get the sticker price. And by mid-1986 they were having to offer the same cash rebates and reduced financing charges that Detroit had been offering for several years.

Detroit also is developing new lower-priced cars with all the features of larger cars. They are being made in partnership with Japanese, Korean, Taiwanese and Brazilian manufacturers. So their production is no comfort to the thousands of American autoworkers laid off in the late 1970s and early '80s.

Meanwhile, the growth of the U.S. economy slowed to a crawl in 1986 with the gain in the gross national product falling to 0.6 percent in mid-summer.

All this adds up to gloom.

I also found many persons deeply concerned over our other areas of foreign involvement, the Middle East and Central America. Very few could see much that was encouraging in either region. The Arab nations, led by Syria and Libya, still show no desire to seek a permanent peace with Israel, and Syria still fans the flames of the bloody guerrilla warfare in Lebanon.

The Arabs think time is on their side, that Israel will be unable to solve its demographic problem—the fact that the Arab birthrate inside Israel is much higher than the Jewish birthrate and immigration of Jews into Israel now is hardly a trickle.

Anti-Americanism clearly is growing still in the Arab world.

Nor could my friends see much hope of a satisfactory end to the Nicaraguan crisis. On the other hand, they seemed to think the chances for an ultimate peaceful settlement in El

Salvador are getting better. Return to the Monroe Doctrine is what most of those I talked to about the hemisphere's problems hoped for.

So where do we stand?

We stand in the midst of chagrin and disappointment and the short-term outlook is very gloomy. But we have been through worse times in our history and have survived and continued to progress. None of the things that are wrong with our policies and tactics are incorrigible. We can correct them all if we make up our minds to. What seems to be incorrigible is the irresponsible and infantile behavior of so many of our politicians. But they can be thrown out of office. That's what makes our country the greatest on earth.

As Franklin Roosevelt said in his first inaugural address, "The only thing we have to fear is fear itself."

Yes, I can see a unified America, working for the common good.

I can see all of us proudly holding our banner high, exclaiming the words, "Give to the world, you just don't live for yourself, and life will be better for all of the people, as the world will give back to you."

CHAPTER 12

# Where to Start

I AM an optimist.

I not only believe that all the contradictory trends in American society and the economy will be corrected, I believe we are on the verge of entering a new era of great prosperity. I don't know how long it will take to make the corrections but I feel sure that the next fifty years will be a period of enormous progress.

There is an astounding amount of prosperity in the nation right now. Very recently a developer announced he would build a new subdivision in New Jersey with the prices of the houses starting at $1 million! Just think a moment about what kind of income a family must have to make a down payment of, probably, $250,000 and carry the mortgage, taxes and insurance on one of those houses.

New Jersey is one state where the luxury real estate market has not collapsed. In plenty of rural areas in the Garden State there are many homes selling for around $450,000 and some for up to $1.5 million. Many of the people who buy those homes pay all cash, no mortgages. Other homes are sold with very low down payments and the huge mortgages are kept afloat by the buyers by means of some very fancy leveraged business operations, some of dubious legality.

The lists of the highest paid corporate executives and the

reports of average compensation for executives in the high technology, financial services and some other industries reveal that there is plenty of wealth in America in spite of our national economic problems.

In January, 1986, *U.S. News & World Report* said that by the end of 1986 there would be one million millionaires in the country, one for every one hundred households and one for every two hundred and forty individuals. About fifteen years ago *Time* magazine reported there were 100,000 millionaires in the land. Of course, inflation accounts for much of this huge increase in millionaires, but there's also a lot of natural growth in the gain.

However, the working class and the middle class are having to struggle to hang on and their immediate outlook is not good.

The place to start correcting the bad policies and philosophies that afflict the nation is in the home.

Of course we need to do what we can to elect better legislators and executives, but real reform must come from grass roots, and that means the home. We need to strengthen family life. I think the best way to accomplish this is for parents to talk with children, especially with teen-agers, about all family financial and moral matters and about political affairs, and we must talk with them as equals, not making authoritarian pronouncements.

The kids know by the time they are ten or eleven that an awful lot, perhaps most, of parental authoritarian statements simply won't hold water. The kids also are way ahead of their parents in willingness to think about and discuss moral, economic and political matters, but most parents don't want to hear what the kids think. That drives the youngsters into the arms of a host of radical theoreticians whose ideas they read about or hear about, and into banding together in demonstrations for causes that have attracted their enthusiasm—mostly good causes, but some that are very misguided.

How many parents ever talk to their children about the intellectual, aesthetic and moral implications of rock and roll music? Mostly they either agree with the kids that the sound is great and some of the ballads tell about life the way it is, or they call all the music and ballads garbage without discussing the whys or wherefores. We also should be interested in the youngsters' preoccupation with ecological problems such as acid rain, and in their fear of war, especially nuclear war. After all, if war comes, they are the ones who will have to do the fighting.

I do not mean to imply that there should not be authority in the home. There should be much more authority but it should be exercised to improve behavior, not to brush off ideas and opinions. Parents should earn the right to exercise authority, not take it for granted. The absence of authority in the home and in the schools growing out of the excessive permissiveness of our society will be the hardest destructive aspect of the present system to correct. In order to correct this cancerous problem, parents must first correct themselves.

Talking with children as equals is not enough. Parents must set good examples for them. That means refraining from extravagance and hedonism, from bitter husband and wife quarrels, from excessive gambling, excessive drinking and "doing drugs" for thrills.

Next, they must give moral backing to the school teachers instead of indignantly and belligerently supporting the rude and rebellious behavior of their children in the classroom and constantly seeking special consideration for their youngsters.

In this connection, we will have to deal firmly with a host of psychologists and some educators who believe (although not publicly) that American society should be ruled by children because the children are instinctively right about most things while grownups are usually wrong because they have been corrupted by experience. That's dangerous hogwash.

The goal should be to rear children who will not be another "me generation" adamant in demanding that the persons they vote into office put their special interests and desires ahead of the general welfare.

A good way for young adults to make a start at a better family life and a better economic future is to decide not to have too many children. This decision should be made not just to curb overpopulation (actually the Census Bureau says we are down as a nation slightly below the replacement rate of two children per couple) but to avoid personal disaster in later years.

For centuries many children were desired partly because so many died in childhood but mainly because the grownup children would care for their parents in their old age. But how many parents have to continue to care for their children all through their middle years and even in their declining years. The Census Bureau says that in 1985, some 19 million, or 28 percent of all persons between the ages of eighteen and thirty-four, were still living with their parents and that this figure has grown very sharply in the past decade. The bureau gives unemployment, multiplying divorces and the housing shortage as the chief reasons for young people remaining with their parents or coming back after leaving the nest. If they are employed, these young adults usually pay their parents for room and board, but many do not, and in any case their presence puts many burdens and impositions on the parents. The situation reminds me of a song that was popular in the late 1930s. A girl who is getting married to the boy next door sings, "We can't live with his folks because his folks are still living with their folks."

A most important decision for young couples is to save. Savings of three to 10 percent of total income should be put away each week. The higher percentage figure is for incomes above about $600 a week. The discipline of this habit is of incalculable moral value and it builds confidence. As soon as the children are old enough to understand they should have the family savings program explained to them clearly and firmly and they should be required to save out of their allowances and any money they earn.

Interest rates paid by banks and other lending institutions on savings deposits have fallen from the peaks of the late 1970s and early '80s but they still are very high compared to those of the good old days, and a much wider variety of savings accounts are available now—insured market rate accounts and a host of certificates of deposit of varying terms and interest rates.

Yet a surprising proportion of the people do not appear to know how much savings accounts can grow. They don't appreciate what I call the miracle of compound interest. That means that the interest earned by your account is added to the principal periodically, often daily, and thus increases the interest earned thereafter. For example, if you put $20 a month into an account that paid 5 percent in straight interest, the account would appreciate by $600 over ten years, but if the interest is compounded the account may earn more than $725 in ten years and in the following decade compounding will run the interest earned up still faster.

Next a decision must be made to avoid the squandermania that has been a plague in our country for almost forty years. Most people who have jobs buy too many things they don't need and may never use. They pay too much for clothing and for automobiles. They do this out of crass and hedonistic materialism. They tell themselves that most of the luxury items are good investments because they will grow in value. The truth is that very few material possessions appreciate in value over the years and those that do usually require meticulous and expensive care. Nor can these things that gain in value be sold in a hurry to raise cash as a rule. The prices of even diamonds and gold and silver objects fluctuate alarmingly and are subject to the whims of fashion that can make them almost worthless for periods of many years.

The consequences of squandermania are not just wasted money. It causes serious physical and mental health problems and leads to many divorces, abandonment of children and not infrequently to suicide.

Squandermania is bound to lead a couple into more debt than they can carry. Often it leads to both financial and social bankruptcy. Nothing is more nerve wracking and humiliating to most of us than being buried under a mountain of debt which we can see no hope of paying off. This can induce acute physical illness, dyspepsia, gastric ulcer and heart problems, or a nervous breakdown on the part of the family breadwinner. It can cause severe personality changes that will make it difficult to keep a job, let alone win promotions.

Some family and marriage counsellors estimate that almost half of all couples that get into hopeless debt soon end up in the divorce courts.

Often, only one partner in the marriage is addicted to squandermania. It often is the husband, but probably more frequently the wife. Some women simply cannot resist the temptation to spend a lot more money than they and their husbands can earn. I recall a sad case from my own experience of a chap who worked at two jobs but still was unable to come near paying off the bills his wife ran up so blithely. When he had exhausted every other loan possibility he asked his employer to lend him money to pay off the debts. The boss, who knew the wife, said: "What's the use? If I bail you out, she'll just do it again, and again."

The upshot was that one day the chap borrowed a pistol and blew his brains out. That's an extreme case, but excessive debt incurred by squandermania or for any other reason ruins millions of marriages and blights the lives of both parents and children.

Financial protection is best provided during the prime years of the family bread winner by a substantial term life insurance policy and every married man should buy as large a policy as he can afford and increase its face amount periodically during his prime years. Protection for the declining years should be by means of savings and investments.

Squandermania, of course, is greatly aggravated by the use of credit cards, which most people consider the most wonderful invention since the wheel, but it enchains families to debt and adds up to 19 percent a year in interest charged on the cost of most products and services. Considering that the new tax law is eliminating most of the deductions for consumer interest payments, credit card interest is going to get very burdensome.

Grey Advertising, which has a very good research department, examined one aspect of squandermania by surveying a sampling of people Grey called the "ultraconsumers," the "people who want the best of everything and want it right now."

The survey showed that many of these ultraconsumers want more than they can afford; 80 percent of them have gross incomes of $25,000 to $40,000 a year. Only 20 percent have gross incomes of $75,000 a year, the sum at which household luxuries become truly affordable under present economic conditions.

The Census Bureau says the average American family owed $6,166 in 1986 over and above mortgage debt. But if that's a population average a lot of people who are debt free must have been counted in calculating it. The average debt of debt-prone families must be much higher.

In spite of the vogue for weight control, many Americans squander money by overeating and not following a reasonably balanced diet. This not only hurts in the pocketbook, it can bring on invalidism and early death.

So, people should avoid squandermania by learning good

buying habits and sternly avoiding impulse buying. You can learn a lot from books about shopping and from the consumers' columns in newspapers and magazines.

But what are we to think of a couple earning $75,000 a year and having one child who tell a reporter for a national magazine they are afraid to have a second child because it would stretch their resources too far? What would a couple raising three kids on a policeman's pay think about that? Obviously, the $75,000-a-year couple want too many luxuries, and they put luxuries ahead of their expressed desire for a second child. They aren't willing to make any sacrifices.

Comparatively soon, the young couple should begin to think about investing in securities, which not only can pay good dividends but can appreciate greatly in value and be sold at a profit. They also can depreciate in value and have to be sold at a loss.

Investing in securities or in almost anything else that might bring substantial gains is venturing into very murky waters, waters much too murky for the average uninformed citizen. And Americans are uninformed because the teaching of economics in our high schools and even in our community colleges usually is poor. Economics is not an exact science, so it can't be taught out of a textbook like mathematics or chemistry. Indeed, most economic textbooks are all unproven theory, the personal ideas of the author, and the writing is far too obscure for high school kids, or even for businessmen. The instructors assigned to teach economics in high school or community colleges seldom have any real knowledge or experience in the field.

So, by the time a couple has saved a nest egg and is ready to invest they may feel the urge to engage a financial planner. This urge should be ignored by most people. They simply don't need a financial planner and a bad one could dissipate their savings rather soon. An adequate term life insurance policy on the breadwinner, and an IRA can be bought without help, and savings can be deposited or invested in good mutual funds.

It's true that a good financial planner might make the nest egg grow, but such a one is very hard to find.

Unfortunately, advising people about financial planning has become a racket. Thousands of phonies and outright sharks have gotten into the act. Many, masquerading as advisors, are really high-pressure salesmen for dubious propositions such as selling shares in apartment buildings that may be converted to co-ops with big profits to the owners. But the "advisor" doesn't tell his client-victims that they also may become liable for some very large additional costs.

The rapid expansion of the financial planning profession has created an urgent need for regulation of the business. In nearly all states, financial planners now are either unregulated or underregulated. This must be corrected. Unless they are graduates of several respected schools in the country offering degree courses in financial planning, those wanting to be planners should be required to pass an examination. All should be licensed and bonded.

Still another important decision is whether to buy a home or live for many years in rented quarters. Until comparatively recent years, home ownership was not usually a paying proposition in the United States. It still is questionable in spite of the big profits many people have made in buying and selling houses in recent years, but the horrible shortage of rental housing makes most families long for a home of their own where they want it, not just where they can find it.

The huge appreciation of the prices of homes in the past two decades makes the sacrifices necessary to buy a house seem much more worthwhile than was the case in the past. However, the rise in value of a house often is not nearly as great as it seems. Take a couple who bought a home thirty years ago for $30,000 and sold it recently for $200,000. That's an apparent profit of $170,000. But the $30,000 that was paid for the house would be nearer $120,000 in today's money. That cuts the true profit to $80,000 in today's money or $20,000 in the money of thirty years ago.

I think renting still may be better than owning a home if suitable quarters can be found at a reasonable rental, but that's a big "if."

The final decision a couple should make is to plan in early middle age for financing ultimate retirement. Of course, Social Security benefits will play a major role in the plan followed by income from investments and savings. Company pensions are unpredictable, so are union pensions. If one becomes a real big shot in a prosperous company, he or she will be able to retire in genuine luxury, but for those who move from job to job a lot and do not have spectacular or exceptional careers, a company pension or a union pension cannot be a big deal even though the federal laws governing the vesting of pensions have been changed greatly in the employee's favor in recent years.

That leaves matters up to what one can do for one's self— savings deposits, investments in securities, tax deferred annuities, Individual Retirement Accounts and mutual funds. Couples should start working on their retirement financing plans as early as possible.

New federal laws also have put some restraints on mandatory retirement, but federal law can't protect you from the simple disappearance of your job as a result of automation or drastic changes in your industry or the general economic situation. Many corporations recently have announced programs to slash their administrative working forces by up to 25 percent. Frequently, they offer early retirement on pensions somewhat smaller than the workers had expected to those being dropped.

I don't know who first said, "This too will pass," but its true about almost everything unpleasant in life. The one thing we can be sure of is that virtually everything changes steadily, and in the two hundred and ten years of the United States' history the changes have invariably been good for the vast majority of the people. There is not the slightest reason to doubt that this will continue to be true. Of course, not every item of change is for the better, many are not, but overall the changes will bring about both economic and social progress.

In Chapter 4 I reported that nearly everybody I talked with on my travels still considered the United States the land of opportunity, The Roper Poll organization recently asked that same question to a sampling of people for *U.S. News & World Report*. Those queried also were asked if tomorrow will be better. The replies were nearly 100 percent "yes" to both questions.

One reason for the optimism, is that the demographic pressures on the economy exerted by those born in the "baby boom" years is subsiding. The "baby boomers" now have been absorbed into the adult working force for the most part. This is so true that companies that rely mainly on teen-age workers encountered a labor shortage in the summer of 1986.

Another reason is that people's expectations are becoming more realistic, and that could bring down American industry's costs considerably. The Congressional Office of Technology and Assessment says that of the 11 million manufacturing workers who lost jobs between 1979 and 1984, half of those who succeeded in finding new jobs had to take pay cuts. That's rough on those individuals, but if it gives Americans a more realistic view of the economic facts of life, it could help lead to better times by helping to make American manufactured products competitive in world markets again.

We now have thirteen years to go until the end of the twentieth century. I predict confidently that by the year 2,000 nearly all of us still living will have forgotten the troubles and problems of the mid-1980s and will be engrossed in making the most of a great new era of progress and prosperity.

# CHAPTER 13

# *Our International Dilemmas*

**B**ECAUSE I found that, throughout the country, people feel that the threat of nuclear war is the greatest peril in the world today and that this poses our greatest foreign policy dilemma, I looked around for some knowledgeable and authoritative information on the subject.

Eventually I obtained an interview with General Vernon Walters, our ambassador to the United Nations. General Walters has been engaged in diplomacy for more than thirty years. He speaks Russian—and six other foreign languages—fluently and has traveled all over the world. I was not surprised when he told me he does not agree with those who live in fear of nuclear war. He sees no real danger of such a conflict.

I will include a full transcript of the interview later in this chapter, but first I want to report on what people I talked with had to say about three other international dilemmas the United States is faced with.

Besides the nuclear weapons problem, I found people most interested in the Central American question—and to the Nicaraguan Contras and the governments in power in El Salvador and Guatemala—in the problem of Israel and the Palestinian refugees and the resulting spread of Arab terrorism, and in our relations with Iran.

The Central American problem aroused the most dispute. Many persons said passionately that we should get out of Central America before it turns into another Vietnam. Others insisted just as passionately that the Russians and Cubans are using Nicaragua as the starting base for a domino strategy that ultimately will expand to Mexico and much of the rest of Latin America if we do not halt the menace now.

Most people tended to blame Fidel Castro for our troubles in Central America, saying that the Cuban dictator is the willing tool of Moscow and always will be. Therefore, it was argued there can be no reasonable settlement of our difficulties in Nicaragua and El Salvador until Castro dies or is overthrown and there is no early prospect of either. But the Central American question is ultimately amenable to a fair solution, it was generally agreed.

The Iranian problem also is soluble, most people said, but not until after the Ayatolah Khomeini disappears from the scene and certainly not while the war between Iran and Iraq drags on. I found absolutely no disposition anywhere in the country to forgive Khomeini for the cruel holding of the fifty-six hostages in the U.S. embassy in Tehran during the last year of the Carter administration.

I didn't find many persons who had an opinion about the Iranian-Iraqui war. Those who did have opinions said we should remain strictly neutral in the conflict. There was general agreement that an early end of the war would be in the interest of the United States but only if neither side won a clear-cut victory. An outright triumph by either side could have a dangerously destabilizing impact on the entire Middle East.

Some persons said the Russians were prolonging the war by providing munitions to both sides and encouraging them to fight on and bleed and bleed. Many said the Soviet Union alone can gain by a prolonged struggle.

I found that many, perhaps most, Americans think the problem of Israel and the Palestinian refugees is altogether insoluble. There still is enormous admiration in our country for the way Jews have built a strong nation in Israel and for their military performance and valor. Even Americans who always have doubted the wisdom of Zionism and the creation of Israel feel that way, but as nearly as I could gather, most see the refugee problem as totally insoluble.

These refugees were not expelled from Israel during the first Arab-Israeli war. They fled because they believed assurances of the Arab states that Israel would be destroyed and then the refugees would return in triumph to reclaim their homes and lands. The Israelis always have claimed that they could not have taken the refugees back after routing the Arab armies and survived as a Jewish state. They still stand on this contention and also say there is no room within the somewhat enlarged borders of Israel for the refugees, whose numbers have much more than doubled since the flight from Palestine. They live in camps and small regions grudgingly alloted them by the Arab states.

The Muslim states never have shown any inclination to accept the refugees as permanent residents and the leaders of the PLO and other refugee factions are bitterly opposed to absorption of their people by any nation. That would destroy the cause for which they fight. This cause and the frustrations growing out of it motivate the Arab terrorists for the most part.

This Israeli-Palestinian guerrilla warfare now has been going on for thirty-eight years and, as matters now stand, it could go on another thirty-eight years with no solution in sight and with continuing outbreaks of terrorism. Even if the Arab states were to defeat Israel in a new war, which is most unlikely, that would not solve the Palestinian trouble because there still would be no room in Israel for the refugees and the large Arab populace already living in Israel would not welcome them. The same thing would be true if the Jews lost control of Palestine by simple demographics—that is, if the higher Arab birthrate and a decline of Jewish immigration enabled the Arab population to engulf the Jews and take over control of the country. There would still be no room for the refugees and their numerous offspring.

So, if the problem goes unsolved, what will happen?

Not many of those I talked with wanted to hazard a guess but those who did said that this large festering wound on world society could only be healed by time and by the decision of individual refugee families to abandon the Palestinian cause as lost forever and seek their own salvation anywhere in the world they can find it.

That process easily could take more than another thirty-eight years.

But the fear of nuclear war remains the chief international issue agitating the American people. I was very lucky in getting the interview with Ambassador Walters and learning his personal views on the issue. General Walters is somewhat unusual for a military man. Born in New York, he was educated in France and England because his father was engaged in international insurance. He followed his father into insurance somewhat reluctantly, but the outbreak of World War II almost wiped out their business. He enlisted in the Army as a private in 1941, and in a career of thirty-five years he rose to the rank of lieutenant-general.

His climb up the military ladder came about partly because of his skill in languages and his study of the art and rules of diplomacy. He served as interpreter and special aide to presidents Truman, Eisenhower and Nixon and to several generals. He served General Alexander Haig while Haig was Nixon's Secretary of State. He had tours of duty in Italy, Brazil, Vietnam and France and as a trouble-shooter for President Reagan with the rank of ambassador-at-large was sent to one hundred and eight countries. Not surprisingly, he has a chest full of ribbons signifying decorations by many governments. He also served as deputy director of the CIA during the Carter administration. He is the author of a couple of books and many magazine articles and book reviews.

He is a Catholic and a conservative. In a recent interview, he stressed the point that Americans should take an "unemotional attitude" towards what he called "friendly" dictatorships. He is not universally admired. Some liberal leaders have characterized him as "an amoral operator."

Henry Kissinger, who said he was "very high on Ambassador Walters," described him as a "modulated" version of Jeane Kirkpatrick, his aggressive predecessor at the United Nations.

And now to the transcript of the interview:

*Milton:* In my travels I have noted that the main concern that people have besides their finances and their families, the AIDS epidemic, crime and all those other things that affect people in their daily lives, is the possibility of nuclear war. Have you found that to be so?

*Walters:* I found it a widespread fear but I personally must tell you that I do not believe there is any serious chance of nuclear war. I am probably one of the very few people still active in the United States government who has seen a nuclear weapon detonated in the atmosphere. I have seen eight of them and this is a very sobering experience and my view is that the Soviet leaders have probably seen them too and understand how insane this would be. And I really do not lose any sleep at night at all over the possibility of a nuclear war— not unless the Soviet Union were run by a madman like Khadafy, which it is not. It is run by someone with whom we disagree in almost every moral, political and economic way you can think of, but he is not a madman. And furthermore I think Stalin probably could have pushed the button alone. I think the Soviet leadership now is of such makeup that no one man can push the button alone and that's a great security for mankind, and we know ourselves all the constraints there are on the president.

*Milton:* But what would happen if a madman like Khadafy did get the bomb?

*Walters:* I don't know what would happen, but he would have to have the means of delivering it, and I think, you know, if it ever became seriously possible, someone would do something. You saw what the Israelis did to the Iraqui act. I mean, there are no secrets about this. When people are working on nuclear weapons people generally know and I think that is one of the rare areas where Soviet and American policy coincide—non-proliferation of nuclear weapons to any more countries.

*Milton:* You know, as you can see by my book, *A Nation Saved: Thank You, President Reagan,* I have been an ardent admirer of our president, and when Gorbachev in his speech yesterday commented among other things that he didn't think there was an eagle in the White House, it kind of bothered me.

*Walters:* He did think there was an eagle in the White House and that's why he is bothered and that's why there was no agreement. He couldn't find a compliant, soft and manipulable man. He found a tough president who knows that his primary responsibility is to the people of America and the survival of human freedom.

*Milton:* And, of course, his constant harping on the SDI. And yet is it because he fears this?

*Walters:* Well, the Soviets have been working on SDI for almost seventeen years. There have been many thousands of people. There have been three administrations in the Soviet Union dedicated to this, over a billion dollars a year. They haven't done very well and they realize that in three years we've gone further than they have in seventeen. And, how anybody can regard a system which is totally defensive in nature as offensive or in some way harmful to another country is difficult for me to understand. The ABM Treaty allows each country to deploy one defensive set of weapons. The Soviet Union has deployed that set around Moscow. But that system functions on the basis of exploding nuclear weapons to prevent incoming missiles. The United States had developed no such system around anything and the whole principle and understanding of SDI does not involve the use of nuclear weapons at any time. So we are talking about two entirely different things.

*Milton:* And even the fact the President Reagan offered almost a partnership on this whole transaction must amaze the rest of the world.

*Walters:* I think it amazes the rest of the world. It makes the Russians very suspicious. Why would he do that? No man in his right mind would do that. They wonder where the trick is. They are incapable of conceiving, thinking about these things the way we do.

*Milton:* Do you think it's at all possible, because there are only two years left to President Reagan's administration, that there will be some terms agreed to on disarmament?

*Walters:* I think there is a fairly good chance that we will reach some kind of arms limitation agreement in the next two years. On the other hand, you know, I cannot probe the Russian mind. They may decide that the best thing for them to do is wait and hope that a Democratic president will be elected who will be more amenable to their views.

*Milton:* Speaking of a Democratic president, I personally doubt that as a possibility.

*Walters:* I do too.

*Milton:* But even if a Republican is president, it's going to be an awful dejection on the part of the citizenry after watching President Reagan for eight years.

*Walters:* Well, President Reagan is both an extraordinarily able president and an extraordinarily charismatic president. I think it is asking too much of the American people that we produce every eight years an extraordinary genius like Ronald Reagan, but I am sure that the creative genius in the American people and their good sense will give us another president who will have the kind of firmness and the kind of toughness that is necessary to lead our country forward into the twenty-first century.

*Milton:* That is the first time I've heard the word "genius" applied to Ronald Reagan and I imagine you sincerely believe that.

*Walters:* I know the man. I watched the man in cabinet meetings. This man is a genius.

*Milton:* Yet some of his critics say he goes to sleep at cabinet meetings.

*Walters:* Well, I remember one day he strolled in a very youthful way and said, "I'll make you one promise. I won't fall asleep during this cabinet meeting." Everybody burst out laughing because they knew how ridiculous that proposition was. He is an extraordinarily vigorous man and I only hope if I get to his age, I'll be in half as good shape as he is—physically, mentally and spiritually.

*Milton:* Not only that, hasn't he been an inspiration to not only all America in boosting patriotism and everything but to the elderly people who look at this man, seventy-five years of age. All the others try to retire at sixty and sixty-five. Many of them, I know, haven't been retiring lately so early.

*Walters:* The thing you've got to understand is that Ronald Reagan has never slacked down. He has continued to serve his country at an age when most people are riding golf carts. He has decided it is his job to serve the American people and I thank God that he made that decision.

*Milton:* What an excellent way of putting it, Ambassador! Just another question, if I may. I have said and I wonder how close you'll agree with me that Ronald Reagan is probably the best president we've had and the most accomplished president for the country since George Washington.

*Walters:* Well, I think that that's probably pretty close to the truth. I find comparisons odious, but I think certainly he is one of the extraordinary American presidents in my lifetime and he has infused the American people with the new and renewed belief in their own future and in their own mighty destiny that they were in the way of losing until he came upon the scene.

*Milton:* Thank you very much. It certainly has been my pleasure to be with you today.

# Epilogue

Nothing great was ever achieved without enthusiasm.

\* \* \*

Hitch your wagon to a star.

—RALPH WALDO EMERSON

**W**hile I have been writing this book something striking has happened.

The recession of 1986 has sharpened with many mergers and big layoffs in industry and large increases in our national budget and trade deficits; but millions of Americans are adapting to the new situation successfully by hard work and intelligence.

This made me remember from my youth that, cruel as the Great Depression of the 1930s was, it also had its good effects on our society. Consequently many people said towards the end of the depression that it actually had been good for the nation in spite of the harsh blows it dealt to so many people. "It chastened us after the follies of the 1920s," was a common observation.

The Great Depression was a social cleansing as well as an economic shake out. It brought families and neighbors closer together. It revised community attitudes from unthinking boosterism to a demand for genuine and broad improvement in the social structure. That improvement ultimately was achieved.

I see the same thing starting to happen now. The recession is shaking people out of smug complacency and the unabashed pursuit of hedonistic living. It is making everyone realize that the psychology of the "me generation" hasn't worked and never can work for long.

Already it is making most people a lot more willing to work hard than was the case in the early 1980s. In accomplishing this, the recession is reviving faith in the work ethic, the ethic that was ridiculed so much in the 1970s. The recession also is causing people to remember that family members, neighbors and friends ultimately are dependent on each other and must help each other when or even before serious trouble strikes.

All this is certain to have good economic effects that will partly offset the cruel impact of layoffs in business and industry. It will bring costs down in both production and the service industries and make us better able again to compete with other nations. By curbing extravagant living habits it should reduce the imports of foreign luxury products and thus help in cutting the trade deficit. But that hasn't happened yet; the trade deficit is still rising.

The recession eventually should have a sharply dampening impact on the frivolity and triviality that has been so marked in American society in recent years.

By pulling families and neighbors closer together, it should make us more conscious of our national identity and the need to preserve it.

In short, it should bring patriotism back into fashion.

It might even bring reading Emerson back into fashion.

Not nearly enough Americans read Emerson today. This is scandalous because he remains our best philosopher and a pretty good poet. High school students used to be required to read some of his essays and poems.

Emerson not only was a great optimist, he was the eternal champion of those virtues of the American spirit we sorely need to renew now. In one of his poems, he said life is too short to waste on being cynical or quarrelsome. In another, he said one must be "too busied with the crowded hour to fear to live or die."

Daily we repeat some of Emerson's more memorable passages without remembering who wrote them, that "all mankind loves a lover," that "a foolish consistency is the hobgoblin of small minds," that "every man is wanted, and no man is wanted much," and that "there is always a best way to do everything, if it be to boil an egg."

Emerson was a fervent patriot, a quality not in favor with today's philosophers and poets. He was patriotic in spite of the fact that the America of his time was more imperialist and aggressive by far than our worst enemies could accuse us of being today. In our day we have not annexed any territories, in fact we have relinquished some, but in Emerson's lifetime we seized Texas and California from Mexico, took Florida from Spain, bought the vast Mississippi Valley from France, bought Alaska from Russia and forced the British into a very favorable (for us) border settlement in the Pacific Northwest.

Emerson's works do not show any great zeal for this expansion. In fact, he said, "I think no virtue goes with size." He simply accepted expansion as an inevitable result of geography, history and economics. His essays are filled with enthusiasm for freedom, justice, truth and courage, and always he is insistent on the importance of good deportment and shows great admiration for fine manners.

We need a lot of Emersons today. They need not be poets,

they could be teachers, clergymen, novelists or business people, perhaps even some politicians.

Of all the popular quotations from Emerson, I think the two I have put at the head of this epilogue are the most apt for our times. We need to consider them together, not separately. There is plenty of enthusiasm in this vast country but not enough of it is hitched to the stars. A great many Americans, young and old, do hitch their wagons to a star, but often to the wrong star.

For example, in the years since World War II, there has been tremendous enthusiasm in the country for racial equality and that is most justified, but many people carry this enthusiasm to misguided extremes, to demands for special racial privileges as compensation for past injustices. In reality a black person is entitled to equality because he or she is an American human being, not to privileges for being black. We must not polarize our large black population and turn it into a minority political bloc. If we do that, the huge Hispanic minority, swelled by illegal immigration, and other minorities also will become political blocs and ultimately we will be fragmented like so many other nations in the world that are so split up that they cannot maintain stable coalition governments, much less majority governments.

Our governmental system was founded on and still depends on majority rule, not coalition rule with its polarized blocs and polarized issues of race, religion and other special interests, creating an inherent instability. That is why proportional representation has never attained much popularity in the United States. So misguided fanatical support for racial privilege is a perfect example of hitching our wagon to the wrong star.

This nation was founded on liberty and it grew and developed on three positive social principles—optimism, altruism and idealism. A lot of negative principles such as greed and ruthlessness also figured in the growth. We need to go back to those three positive principles and we need to apply them to everything we do—to education, to the legal system, to business and everyday living and to our relations with other nations.

We have some mistaken ideas now about the meaning of idealism and altruism. We tend to think both these words mean being soft and lenient. We should remember the Pilgrims of New England. They were extremely idealistic but they were tough, strict and vigorous in enforcing the law at all times. They believed in the whipping post and the gallows. They were rather pigheaded in much of their religious philosophy but they did leave us the heritage of a strong and moral people whose descendants became firm believers in a democratic society.

We also should remember how rapidly life and what we call "the system," which so many persons, especially young people, deride with much justice, change in America. "The system" reflects the complicated conditions of everyday life so it has to change rapidly. This change is so rapid that 90 percent of us do not perceive it, much less take advantage of it. How many of us living today could, at a moment's notice, sit down and write an accurate description of life in America in the early 1970s? Very few, I imagine.

The big lesson we should learn from Emerson is that, even for such a sophisticated intellectual as he was, patriotism, the emotional side of Americanism, is paramount. We should reintroduce the emotion of patriotism in our schools from grammar school through the universities. Let us restore the salute to the flag and the pledge of allegiance and a proper observance of Independence Day, Memorial Day and Washington's Birthday.

An obvious reason for doing this is that patriotism breeds optimism and determination. People cannot be optimistic unless they want to be, and patriotism makes them want to be optimistic.

I have continued my travels and lecturing while writing this book and lately I have noticed the acceptance by people I

meet of the realities of the 1986 recession and the promptness
with which most of them came to terms with these realities. I
encountered very little evidence of panic, only a quick decision on the part of most people to roll up their sleeves and get
to work and overcome their problems, and a desire to help
their less fortunate neighbors.

With that attitude prevailing in the population, we are
bound to succeed and soon enter a new era of progress and
prosperity.

My travels around the country and my many talks with so
many people confirmed a number of my favorite observations—my own and those of other people—about human nature and this country:

\*    \*    \*

Ninety percent of winning is being excited.
Everybody wants to be somebody.

—ART WILLIAMS

\*    \*    \*

As to your friends and associates, when in doubt, leave
them out.

\*    \*    \*

The patient investor gets compounded.
The impatient investor gets confounded.

\* \* \*

Everyone must take charge of their own lives.
Drugs destroy hopes and opportunity.

\* \* \*

You cannot do anything about the length of your life, but
you can do something about its width and depth.

\* \* \*

It ain't over till it's over.

—YOGI BERRA

\* \* \*

Give to the world the best that you have
And the best will come back to you.

—CATHARINE WRIGHT

\* \* \*

Your prescription for personal growth in our growing
country should involve second and third opinions.

\*   \*   \*

It is not the critic who counts, not the man who points out
how the strong man stumbled, or where the doer of deeds
could have done them better. The credit belongs to the
man who is actually in the arena; whose face is marred by
dust and sweat and blood; who strives valiantly, who errs
and comes short again and again; who knows the great
enthusiasms, the great devotions, and spends himself in a
worthy cause; who, at the best, knows in the end the
triumph of high achievement; and who, at the worst, at
least fails while daring greatly, so that his place shall never
be with those cold and timid souls who know neither
victory nor defeat.

—THEODORE ROOSEVELT

\*   \*   \*

Money matters—and you better believe it!

\*   \*   \*

Thomas Jefferson wrote: "We hold these truths to be self-
evident, that all men are created equal, that they are
endowed by their Creator with certain inalienable rights,
that among these are life, liberty and the pursuit of
happiness. . . ." I would add: "And the right to pursue
financial independence."

\*   \*   \*

The people and their over-indulgence in plastic card spending have caused much financial indigestion, leading to physical and mental illness and actually aiding the divorce rate.

\*   \*   \*

### PEOPLE POWER

We now live in a world of deflation and it will affect everybody. It is no longer possible to pass on increased costs from bad management and non-productivity to the consumer. The old cliché "Let the Buyer Beware" has been changed by educated consumers; it is now "Let the Competition Beware."

\*   \*   \*

Consumers are more knowledgeable, aggressive in their thoughts and grossly inquisitive about their future than they ever used to be.

\*   \*   \*

Liberty is the right of the individual to stand up for his rights.

\*    \*    \*

The only limitations on our realization of tomorrow is the
limitation which we, by our lack of faith, limited vision and
doubt of the future, impose today.

—ELLIS ARNALL

\*    \*    \*

### AN ADMIRABLE MAN

*If a man is honest with others
    and with himself . . .
If he receives gratefully and gives quietly . . .
    If he is gentle enough to feel
and strong enough to show his feelings . . .
    If he is slow to see the faults of others
        but quick to discover their goodness . . .
If he is cheerful in difficult times
    and modest in success . . .
If he does his best to be true to his beliefs . . .
    Then he is truly an admirable man.*

\*    \*    \*

Money, or even power, can never yield happiness unless it
be accompanied by the goodwill of others. I know a very
clever business man who is making a great deal of money,
mostly by practices which are strictly legal but which have
as their object the outwitting, and the outbargaining, not to
say the hoodwinking, of others. He is less happy than
almost anyone else I know.

—B.C. FORBES

\* \* \*

When I have to do any selling—and all of us are salesmen
in one sense or another—I try to say, not as much as
possible, but as little as is necessary to get the other man
started talking, and then I encourage him to say whatever
is on his mind. Almost everybody likes to talk. Nobody
likes to be talked at. Let your prospect have the floor. Say
just enough to arouse his interest and get him to ask
questions. Your job is to tell him what he wants to know,
not to bore him with a stereotyped patter-patter of words
which are ground out as if from a hurdy-gurdy organ, so
metallic do they ring.

—B.C. FORBES

\* \* \*

You don't live for yourself. You live to make life better
for other people.

—DR. SABIN

\* \* \*

There is an eternal law of compensation. This law was
proclaimed of old in these words: "As ye sow, so shall ye
reap." The wise man will choose to do his exertion while
he is young, while hardship and fatigue and self-denial sit
lightly on his forehead and daunt not his spirit. Every
human being must put something into the world before he
can hope to get all he reasonably needs out of the world—
even millionaires' offspring are less exempt from this
decree than we sometimes are tempted to imagine. If you
begin by denying yourself nothing the world later is apt to
do your denying for you.

—B.C. FORBES

\* \* \*

The American free-enterprise system is like none other
in the world. Everyone has to the opportunity to plant
his or her own *Fortune Tree.*
To the tens of millions of my fellow Americans to whom
money matters seem an awesome obstacle, the preceding
pages can alert them to their true financial value. Building
your house of financial independence is a very individual
endeavor and the degree of your success will be directly
related to your motivations as you travel down life's road.


\*  \*  \*  \*  \*  \*  \*  \*  \*  \*  \*  \*  \*  \*  \*  \*  \*